DESIGN FOR DIGNITY

Studies in Accessibility

DESIGN FOR DIGNITY

Studies in Accessibility

William L. Lebovich

John Wiley & Sons, Inc.
New York • Chichester • Brisbane • Toronto • Singapore

Library of Congress Cataloging-in-publication Data

Lebovich, William L.
    Design for Dignity: studies in accessibility / William L.
Lebovich.
        p.   cm.
    Includes index.
    ISBN 0-471-56910-0
    1. Architecture and the physically handicapped—United States.
I. Title.
NA2545.P5L35   1993
720'.42'0973—dc20   93-3310

Printed in the United States of America
10 9 8 7 6 5 4 3 2 1

For Karen, Jennifer, and Andrew

CONTENTS

FOREWORD

Bill Lebovich has performed an important and timely service in preparing these richly illustrated case studies of diverse environments that promote and enhance the independence and integration of people with disabilities. He shows quite clearly that flexibility, creativity, and imagination are the essential tools for inclusion of people with disabilities in American society—and in fulfilling the promises of the Americans with Disabilities Act of 1990.

Making accommodations is not new, however. In 1787, Benjamin Franklin, a Pennsylvania delegate to the Constitutional Convention and, at 81, the oldest delegate, was virtually unable to walk because of gout, and even slight movement could cause pain from a bladder stone.

So the City of Philadelphia provided four prisoners to carry Franklin between his home and the convention in a sedan chair, which was suspended between two long, slightly flexible poles that damped any bouncing. It must have been an amazing sight as they moved along the streets and up the steps of the State House (later renamed Independence Hall) where the convention sessions were held.

And Franklin frequently wrote out his speeches, and had them read by another delegate, because standing was difficult and uncomfortable.

Franklin's disability was no bar to his contribution—deeply respected by his colleagues, of keen intelligence, calm temper, and good humor, he helped forge the compromises that made agreement on the U.S. Constitution possible. Indeed, William Pierce of Georgia described Franklin as "possess[ing] an activity of mind equal to a youth of twenty-five years of age."

Like Franklin's chair, since ancient times people have used various "assistive devices" to remedy disability, or tried other means to restore lost abilities. But over the past 30 years another, complementary approach to disability and disability solutions has emerged—one that recognizes that disability is not solely a function of an individual's physical or mental impairment, but an interaction between a person's impairment and his or her environment.

Environments can disable—or enable. For example, for the person who uses a wheelchair, steps can prevent entering or moving about a building, but ramps, elevators, and lifts make it accessible. Or for a person with limited vision, a large print menu—a simple accommodation—can allow easy and unassisted selection of a meal.

The Americans with Disabilities Act (ADA), which I was proud to support in the Congress, makes accessibility and accommodations national policy and federal law. Although prior legislation (going back as far as 1968) had a similar purpose, ADA provides a broader mandate and stronger and more certain enforcement.

ADA's stated purpose is "to establish a clear and comprehensive prohibition of discrimination on the basis of disability." To understand ADA, and the sometimes unfamiliar meaning of the word "discrimination" in the context of disability, it is essential to appreciate two principles at its heart.

First, fundamental convictions about human equality and the rights inherent in *all* individuals, including people with disabilities, and society's responsibility to protect those rights. As the Declaration of Independence proudly and forcefully proclaims: "We hold these truths to be self-evident, that all men are created equal, that they are endowed by their Creator with certain unalienable Rights, that among these are Life, Liberty, and the Pursuit of Happiness."

Second, that accessibility and accommodations are not simply matters of personal convenience for people with disabilities, but are essential if they are to be productive and active citizens. And to deny accessibility and accommodations is discrimination—and with ADA, unlawful.

Now, no one likes mandates, or to be told what to do. Yet I have been repeatedly impressed with the enthusiasm and good cheer of so many I have met—state and local officials, businessmen and women—who are doing what is needed to make ADA work.

What is their motivation? I believe because they know that it is right and important, and doing the right thing feels good. Also perhaps because disability is so personal—Republican or Democrat, rich or poor, of whatever ethnic background—it affects all of us and our families.

And, of course, any one of us, at any time, can be recruited into the ranks of the disabled—as I learned almost 50 years ago when shrapnel plowed into my right shoulder.

I encourage each reader to study these cases closely, and to note another important, if unstated message: that "universal design"—the term used to describe environments built to the needs of people with *and* without disabilities—not only enables the disabled, but improves the comfort, productivity, and safety of all persons.

Senator Bob Dole

ACKNOWLEDGMENTS

I am grateful for partial support given by Professional Imagining, Eastman Kodak Company.

It is an honor to have a foreword by Senator Bob Dole.

Nearly everyone I spoke with was very generous with his or her time and recommendations. Of course there were some people that I called more often and to whom I owe a special debt. Rick Dudley gave me invaluable leads and insights, and was always available. George Covington frequently shared with me his unique perspective. Marian Vessels, aide to the Maryland Governor for the Americans with Disability Act, spent several hours discussing Baltimore Washington Airport and Orioles Park at Camden Yards, showing me around the latter and good naturedly posing for photographs. Kim Beasley, AIA, at the Paralyzed Veterans of America, gave me many hours of his time, as did John Salmen, AIA, and Jim DiLuigi, AIA, both at Universal Designers & Consultants, Inc. Bonnie Baugh was very helpful on the numerous times I called on her. Maureen West, R.N, Legislative Assistant to Senator Dole, put me in touch with the right people, gave me much helpful information, and smoothed out some otherwise insurmountable problems. Lisa Fricke and Alexander Vachon, also from Senator Dole's staff, were always quite helpful. I asked much of Vicky Rugo of Sasaki Associates and she was always very cooperative and extremely competent.

The first person I discussed this book with was Doug Gordon at the American Institute of Architects, who stayed actively involved, read everything I wrote, reviewed every photograph, and, with his own minimalist style, kept me encouraged. Doug played a critical role, especially when I was first trying to conceptualize this book and he brought the idea to John Wiley & Son's Dan Sayre. Dan, his assistant, Tracy Thornblade, and other editors reviewed the manuscript and photographs with a care and sensitivity that an author and photographer can only dream of. Dan also showed great patience.

No less valuable, merely imposed on less often, were Liz Savage, at Disabilities Rights Education and Defense Fund, Eleanor and Ray Lewis, Professor Joseph Wiedel and Professor Chai Feldblum. In addition to Doug Gordon, several other people at the American Institute of Architects helped me: Michael Jack, Doug's editorial assistant, Bob Peck, who enthusiastically supported the concept of this book and Doug's involvement, Mark Scher, and the AIA Library staff which has always been helpful, especially, Carol Twombly, Jenni Woolums, and Judy Marks. The American Foundation for the Blind's Edward Rush and Elga Joffee were helpful. At the Access Board, David M. Cappozi, Julie Zirlin, Marsha Mazz, and Ruth Lusher (Lusher is now at the Justice Department) were also helpful. Other federal officials who aided me were Special Agent Albert Windham, John Dawson at the Old Executive Office Building, Judith Brotman at the Department of Labor, Catherine Fitts at the Supreme Court, Ursula Hennessy at the Postal Service, Paula Terry at the National Endowment for the Arts, the Forest Service's Joe Meade and David Sherman, Richard Sheppard, Dale Brown, and Dick Dietl at the President's Committee on the Employment of People with Disabilities, and the Department of Education's Rhonda Weiss, David Berkowitz, Dawn Hunter, and Larry Ringer. Carol Lewis at the Maryland Rehabilitation Center, industrial designer Jim Mueller, Professor Wolfgang F. E. Preiser, and the Smithsonian Institution's Jan Majewski, Laurie Trippett, Carla Borden, Caroline Mortimer, and Diane Pilgrim all made invaluable contributions. Janet and Steve Chitwood and their colleagues Carolyn Beckett and Deidre Hayden at Parent Education Advocacy Training Center, along with Lisa Baach were very helpful in explaining the issues concerning the education of children with disabilities. Montgomery County (MD) officials Maggie Roffee, Betsy Luecking, Ellen Masciocchi, June Morganstern, and Gunther Lerche (the latter two are in the School Department) gave me a local perspective. Diane Carstens discussed with me the needs of the elderly. Concerning the process for creating and revising ANSI A117.1, Joe Fruscione at the American National Standards Institute and Robert Spangler at the Council of American Buildings Officials answered my questions. Virginia Stern at the American Association for the Advancement of Science, Elaine Ostroff and Richard Duncan at Adaptive Environment Center, and Jim Hollahan and Sally Weiss at the United Cerebral Palsy Associations also were helpful. Louise Emquist at National Rehabilitation Information Center was especially helpful and Aline Martinez at the American Society of Landscape Architects gave me several citations. Jim Johnson and Bill Bushong shared with me their research on federal accessible design. Barbara Judy explained the Job Accommodation Network to me and gave me the names of some excellent people. Doctors Robert Gerwin, Kim Gibson, and Samuel Ornstein shared their viewpoints with me. Other people who could be mentioned in this paragraph are instead mentioned below with the particular case study they are associated with.

Architects Mary Oehrlein, FAIA; Robert Dale Lynch, AIA; Chris Lethbridge, AIA; Eleanor Krause, AIA; Kent Cooper, AIA; Bill Leckey, AIA; Warren Cox, FAIA; John Forney, Tom Davies, AIA; David Deyell, AIA; Jim Franklin, FAIA; and designers Susan Carter, Katherine McGuiness, and Jane Wallace discussed with me their work in accessible design. John McEwen at the Paper Mill Playhouse, historians Nancy Witherell and Philip Seitz (the latter at the American Academy of Otolaryngology–Head and Neck Surgery), Wendy Jacobs at the Society for the Advancement of Travel for the Handicapped, Harold Barley at Washington Metropolitan Area Transit Authority, and his consultant, Linda Sussman, Michael Oestereicher at Challenges Unlimited, Marge Kumacki at Children's Hospital, Jed Nitzberg at the Hospital for Sick Children (both hospitals in Washington,DC), John Lord at Mobil Oil, Aline Lenaz at Princeton University, Mrs. Miriam King, Curt Sloan, Shawn McDermitt at Paralyzed Veterans of America all provided valuable information. Barrier Free Environment's Lucy Harber and Leslie Young told me about their firm's projects. Had the American Civil Liberties Union started its project to make its Washington headquarters accessible it would have been included; the ACLU's Linthia Gibson was very cooperative.

The following people were directly involved in the specific accessibility studies, provided me with invaluable help, and several very generously gave permission to be photographed:

Chapter 1   Edward's Room
Magenta Yglesias, ASID.

Chapter 3   National Association of Home Builders' Demonstration House
June Prescop, Barry Rosengarten, Dave Williamson (HUD), and the NAHB for permission to reproduce plans.

Chapter 4   Accessible Apartment Bathroom
Susan Dynes.

Chapter 5   Accessible Paths
Lawrence V. Frank, ASLA.

The homeowners in Chapters 1, 2, and 5 were very gracious in their cooperation, but specifically asked not to be identified.

Chapter 6   Gallaudet University
Mickey Fields, AIA, Carol Parr, Charles Mann, Gina Oliva, Muriel Strassler, and Professor Joseph Wiedel (University of Maryland) and Eleanor Krause, AIA.

Chapter 7   Judith A. Resnik Elementary School
Principal Mary Ann Britain, facility planner Deanna Newman, and Thomas Clark, AIA (and for permission to reproduce plans).

Chapter 8   Henry Viscardi High School
Glenn Goldberg and Joseph Russo both at the National Center for National Center for Disability Services, and Angelo Francis Corva, AIA, and Ze'ev Silberman, RA (and for permission to reproduce plans).

Chapter 9   Schools for People with Visual Disabilities
Kenneth Stuckey (Perkins),Thaddeus Neumann and Karen Lubieniecki (Columbia Lighthouse), Street Thoma (and for permission to reproduce his model) and Allison Burrows (Helen Keller).

Chapter 10   National Rehabilitation Hospital and the Washington Home and Hospice
Edward Eckenhoff, Price Baum, Jan Galvin, Betsy Phillips, Lisa O'Keefe (all at National Rehabilitation Hospital), Theodore Mariani, FAIA; Donna Arbogast and Dr. Jared Falek (Washington Home and Hospice), Steve Mackler of the Landscape Group, and Pascal Pittman, AIA of Oudens & Knoop Architects (and for permission to reproduce plans).

Chapter 11   Museum of Science
Betty Davidson, Larry Ralph, and Carolyn Kirdahy.

Chapter 12   The Smithsonian Institution
Mary Grace Potter, Cynthia Field, and Amy Ballard (Smithsonian), Sue Kohler and Jose Martinez (Fine Arts Commission) and Ralston Cox (Advisory Council).

Chapter 13   National Building Museum
Melissa McLoud, David Chase, A. J. Pietrantone (NBM), Edward Ruch (American Foundation for the Blind), R. Steven McCormick and Andrea Mones O'Hara (General Services Administration), Thomas Striegel, AIA (of Davis Buckley, architect for National Law Enforcement Officers Memorial) and Emanuel Mevorah (Washington Metropolitan Area Transportation Authority).

Chapter 14   National Park Service
Robie Lange, Lois Lema, David Park, Kay Ellis, Joy M. Pietschmann, Randy Biallas, AIA, Joanne Blacoe, and Michael Alderstein, AIA (and for permission to reproduce Independence Park brochures).

Chapter 15   Historical Society of Washington
Jane North and Candace Shireman (Society), Baird Smith, AIA (with Geier Brown, Renfrow at the time of the project), and EA-Mueller Consulting Engineers (for permission to reproduce the plan).

Chapter 16   Arena Stage and Shakespeare Theatre
Betty Siegel, Jeri Esocoff Zimmerman, Martha Ingel, and Wayne White and for permission to quote(Arena); Vicky Hoover (Harry Weese Associates, for clippings and permission to reproduce plans); Patricia Boatner (Shakespeare); Richard Madsen, FAIA, and Richard Backer (Graham Gund Architect and the Gunwyn Company).

Chapter 17   Orioles Park at Camden Yards
Kim I. McCalla (Stadium Authority), Gertrude Jeffers, Diane Ebberts, and Marian Vessels (Maryland government); Roy Sommerhof (Orioles); Tom Heiderer; Kim Beasley, AIA.

Chapter 18   St. Elizabeth and Baltimore Hebrew
Father Frederick Bloom and Sanford Cohen.

Chapter 19   Chinn Aquatics & Fitness Center
Peggy Delinocci, Mary Ann Burke, and Pam Sneed, CTRS (Prince William County Park Authority); Dick Murphy (Prince William County Library) and Sharon Wise (Prince William County government); Bill Burrough and Jack Snyder (Montgomery County Recreation); Sasaki Associate's Alan Resnick, AIA, Laura Bobeczko, and Vicky Kayser Rugo (and for permission to reproduce plans); and Jeannie Barrell of the National Recreation & Park Association for permission to quote.

Chapter 20   Waterfront Park
Bill Turner and Amanda Barton (Park Department); Sasaki Associates' Stuart Dawson, FASLA, Varoujan Hagopian, and Vicky Rugo (and for permission to quote and to reproduce plan).

Chapter 21   Mountain Laurel Trail
Roy Geiger, Jr. and Stephanie Sklar (and for permission to reproduce plan).

Chapter 22   Baltimore Washington International Airport
Wilfred Jackson; Carol Riley and Richard Keen (Maryland Aviation Administration, and for permission to reproduce the plan); Pamela Pflueger (Corporate Services for the Deaf); Art Kosatka (Airports Association Council, Int.); Ira Laster (U.S. Department of Transportation); and David Andrews (National Federation for the Blind) for permission to quote his excellent remarks.

Chapter 23   Hyatt Regency Reston
Dianne Murphy and Alicia Angone.

Chapter 24   Cheesecake Factory
Linda Candioty and Russell Werth; and Sandra Gordon of the National Easter Seal Society for permission to quote from a Society brochure.

Chapter 25   The Paralyzed Veterans of America Headquarters
Kim Beasley, AIA, and his colleagues at the PVA.

Chapter 26   Hubert H. Humphrey Park and Friendship Heights Village Center
Leslie Strathmann; Michael C. Poness, AIA, of Walton Madden Cooper, Inc. and for permission to reproduce plans.

Chapter 27   Accessible Paths to Offices
Arthur May, FAIA; Jeffrey Love, AIA (Carr Co.); Eric Johnson (Ward-Hale Design Associates); Margaret Arnold, Ted Bobrow, and Robert DeFillippo (American Association of Retired Persons); and Mark Lewis (National Organization on Disability).

Chapter 28 Great Hall at the Department of Justice Building
Jim Bennett and Anna Franz, AIA (Justice Department); Ginny Thornburgh; Jane Barton; Amy Weinstein, AIA.

Chapter 29 United States Capitol
Jim Ellison, FAIA, and William Ensign, FAIA (Office of the Architect of the Capitol); Deborah Jans (Congressional Special Services); Janet Dorsey (Deputy Postmaster, Senate); Office of the Sargent at Arms (for permission to reproduce tactile map in the public domain); Mark Buse of Senator McCain's office; Maureen West (and for permission to quote Senator Dole's letter); George Covington; and Professor Joseph Wiedel.

Chapter 30 Vice President's Residence
George Covington, Alan Meyers, AIA (Bucher Meyers Polniaszek Silkey + Associates), Carolyn Reynolds Washington, Steven Dick (Naval Observatory), John Dawson, Gail Cleere, and Glen Liener.

Chapter 31 United States Equal Employment Opportunity Commission
Linda Sye, Chip Mace, Pat Higgs, Deidre Davis, Christopher Bell, and Susan Taylor (EEOC); Lida Dersookian, IBD (Leo A Daly) for permission to reproduce the plan; and Richard Sheppard (President's Committee on the Employment of People with Disabilities).

When I started this project, Andrew and Jennifer would ask me, with excited anticipation, when I was going to be done. Over time, the question was asked with a tone much closer to anxiousness. Repeatedly and increasingly frequently, Karen had to assure them that I was almost done and that I would regain my composure. Karen, Jennifer, and Andrew were saints and made this book, like everything else, worthwhile.

Section I

INTRODUCTION

When Abraham Lincoln signed the congressional charter for Gallaudet College for the deaf in 1864, he started a process that culminated with President Bush signing the Americans with Disabilities Act (ADA) on July 26, 1990. Although the ADA has its origins in the nineteenth century, it embodies a far different philosophy toward people with disabilities than would have been seen at that time. People with disabilities were once viewed as being less capable and to be pitied. To the limited degree they were cared for, educated, and employed, it was in a segregated setting. The Americans with Disabilities Act mandates the elimination of physical and cultural barriers that prevent the full integration of people with disabilities into the larger American society.

The direct and immediate antecedents of the ADA are the federal legislation of the last 25 years—the Architectural Barriers Act (1968), The Rehabilitation Act of 1973, The Education of the Handicapped Act (1975, and reauthorized in 1990 as the Individuals with Disabilities Education Act), and the Fair Housing Act of 1988, among others—that attempted to eliminate those barriers. Slightly earlier, in 1961, the American National Standards Institute published its first standard to make buildings accessible. With the newest revision published at the end of January 1993, ANSI A117.1 is the basis for the Uniform Federal Accessibility Standards (1985), the Fair Housing Act's accessibility standards, and the ADA's accessibility standards. (The latter were published as the appendix to the regulations for the Americans with Disabilities Act in the *Federal Register*, July 26, 1991, Part III, Department of Justice, Office of the Attorney General, 28 CFR Part 36, *Nondiscrimination on the Basis of Disability by Public Accommodations and in Commercial Facilities; Final Rule.*) As the existing federal laws and local building codes were insufficient to remove barriers, the Americans with Disabilities Act and its accessibility guidelines were necessary. The guidelines are not a guide to good design; they are only intended to establish minimum standards for physical accessibility. But they are the starting point for creating good design that is accessible.

Language, as well as the legislation, pertaining to people with disabilities has changed dramatically. It is now appreciated that once common terms were derogatory, condescending, pitying, and that they emphasized a person's disability. Even the harsh sound of the words—*handicapped, retarded, spastic*—reinforced, unconsciously, the perception that people with disabilities were separate from, and inferior to, the rest of society. The phrase "a person who uses a wheelchair" is less harsh in sound and meaning than "a wheelchair-bound person," and it places the emphasis on the person rather than on his or her disability. In the same vein, to describe a 3-foot-wide passage as "accessible to someone in a wheelchair" rather than as "wheelchair accessible," places the design concern where it belongs—on the person rather than on the hardware he or she uses.

Perhaps because a person in a wheelchair is the universal symbol of accessibility, many people, without giving it any thought, assume that there is a homogeneous disabled population, consisting almost entirely of people in wheelchairs. Often overlooked are the individuals with hearing, visual, learning, developmental, cognitive disabilities; multiple disabilities; or those with other types of mobility disabilities.

Long-established habits of language and perception concerning people with disabilities cannot be changed by legislation, but the passage of the ADA has made disability a national issue. As a major civil rights act, with unknown financial and legal effects on businesses and governments, and as the means for creating a national building code for accessibility, the ADA has captured an unprecedented degree of interest from the building industry, designers, businesses, local governments, disability advocates, and lawyers. But the interest seems too long stuck in understanding the mind-numbing, creativity-dulling legal and code aspects of the minutiae of the regulations and of the accessibility guidelines.

Good accessible design starts with equal access: not with adding an accessible entrance at the rear while the front entrance remains inaccessible. Equal access extends through the building and provides a person with any type of disability or disabilities the same experiences and the same information that a nondisabled person enjoys. For example, a person in a wheelchair can sign in at a reception desk that has a portion of the counter lowered. In an equal-access building, he or she can move throughout the building, conveniently use any bathroom, and sit with a companion in any section of the auditorium or ballpark. Through pre-performance tours, audiotapes, braille or enlarged print script summaries, and special descriptive broadcasts, the person who is blind or visually impaired can enjoy the theater as much as the nondisabled or the person with a hearing disability who watches the sign interpreters or listens on amplified headphones.

Captioned movies, enlarged or tactile maps and models, audio as well as visual information displays, and physically accessible features open museums and other educational or recreational facilities to previously excluded people. By avoiding the needlessly complex and by creating logical spatial organization, which is strongly articulated and augmented with informative signage (visual and audible), designers make buildings and outdoor spaces more comprehensible to people with developmental, cognitive, and visual disabilities, enabling them to travel more easily and more independently. Through barrier-free architecture, flexible design of adjustable, modular furniture, and the accommodation of assistive technology specific to the individual's needs, more people are mainstreamed into schools and offices.

The most inspiring of the projects to be discussed in the pages that follow were a new building (Orioles Park at Camden Yards) in which providing maximum accessibility was an important design issue and an architectural landmark (the Smithsonian Castle) that was made accessible. In Orioles Park, in fact, the accessibility concerns generated the most architecturally impressive qualities of the building. In the historic Smithsonian Castle, very few, if any, visitors would even notice the physical and information accessibility modifications made. Only fanatics who will not accept any changes to a building would be bothered by this building's accessibility modifications. Respecting the integrity of a historic building (or a pristine landscape) while providing accessibility is the most daunting challenge of accessible design and, perhaps, the most rewarding.

Attitude and personal involvement were critical in achieving accessibility in the case studies. Neither the client nor the designer appeared to have viewed accessibility as a code issue, but rather as a design challenge to assure that people with disabilities could use the facility with dignity. Even when the Uniform Federal Accessibility Standards were the designer's primary guide, people with disabilities influenced the design by their recommendations. Perhaps just their presence made the designer more attuned to providing dignified accessibility. Most importantly, the belief that accessibility is not a static goal, but rather a process that can always evolve, characterizes most of the managers of the facilities studied.

In a different context, John Summerson wrote "It is time for the architect to take a new and more positive view of his functions, to learn to study not merely minimum requirements, but maximum possibilities . . . " (*Heavenly Mansions and Other Essays on Architecture*, W. W. Norton & Co., Inc., New York, 1963, p. 218). His words are, however, especially applicable to architects and other designers concerning accessible design. Accessibility offers the same maximum possibilities for challenging, pleasing, uplifting solutions as any other design problem. And few other design issues are driven by such lofty principles as those of the Americans with Disabilities Act.

Section II

HOMES

Private homes are not covered by either the Americans with Disabilities Act or the Fair Housing Act of 1988, but they are subject to state and local building codes which often incorporate ANSI standards, including ANSI A117.1, which pertains to accessibility. Of the five houses and one bathroom profiled in this section, the sole accessibility concern is for someone in a wheelchair, with the exception of the National Association of Homebuilders'(NAHB) model home. It includes visible and vibrating bed fire alarms for people with hearing disabilities, and door and window handles that can be operated by someone with minimal strength and dexterity.

The NAHB home also differs from the other case studies in that it is intended as a demonstration house, to show that an average sized, average priced prefabricated house can meet the standards for fire safety and accessibility and not look different from other houses. Although people with disabilities and disability experts (they are not synonymous) consulted with the NAHB on the house, it was not designed for a specific individual with a disability, but for the eventuality that as people age, they are more likely to need accessible features.

The other houses and the bathroom discussed in this section reflect the particular needs of specific individuals with disabilities. With the exception of Susan Dynes's bathroom, all the rooms are also used by family members who are not disabled. Therefore, in these homes and in almost all accessible designs, solutions that work at the expense of nondisabled users are not acceptable.

Chapters 1 and 5 discuss accessibility for children in wheelchairs. The parents' concerns were primarily for the children's immediate needs, rather than for features that would also work when the children grew and/or had mastered more physical skills. No national standards exist for designing accessible features scaled to a child's dimensions, so the parents depended on their knowledge and the guidance in one case of their interior designer and in another of their landscape architect. Also, each of the children has very different abilities, so each design had to reflect the child's specific needs, rather than general assumptions about the characteristics of a child in a wheelchair. In only one of the houses is there any exterior indication (a slight curbcut) that the house has an occupant in a wheelchair.

This desire for inconspicuous accessible design was paramount at the NAHB house and at the doctor's house and grounds discussed in Chapter 2. The slate ramp to the front door at the doctor's house and landscaping there do not look like they were designed for someone in a wheelchair. In fact, the ramp might be too steep for someone pushing himself in a wheelchair; but the doctor operates a battery-powered wheelchair.

The wheelchair, which he controls with a toggle switch, is but one of the assistive technologies the doctor employs, which include his very high-tech van (see Chapter 27), a less sophisticated headphone so he does not have to hold his office telephone, easily held U-shaped holders permanently attached to appliances, and several remote controls mounted within easy reach next to his bed. By having as many devices as possible, from the TV to the room thermostat, controlled by remotes, he minimizes the number of times he must go to the considerable effort of getting out of bed once he has settled in at night.

The doctor did not use an architect, designer, or disability expert to design the features he needed. Because he completely understood his needs, he could precisely articulate them, and he had the finances to fulfill them. Susan Dynes, an architectural designer, had the same understanding of her needs as well as the technical ability to design the architectural solutions. The other homes discussed in this section were designed by architects or designers with assistance from the homeowners.

The range of abilities, life styles, financial resources, and long-term goals of the families and the person with the disabilities, as well as the wide variation in specific accessibility features reflects the diversity of the larger nondisabled and disabled population. Even when minimal accessibility standards can be specified, as at the NAHB model house, the specifications are subject to change according to the specific needs of the occupant with a disability.

Chapter 1

EDWARD'S ROOM

Limitless outer space is the decorative theme of Edward's room. The posters are of distant planets, and, when the room was first created for a decorators' show house, a painted metal floor panel simulated the rocky terrain of the moon. Mirrors behind the built-in bookshelves make the space within the room seem boundless. The attention to decoration, and especially this theme of infinite space, is surprising as Edward, 7 years old, who uses a wheelchair, lacks sight.

Magenta Iglesias, ASID, designed "Eddie's Room" for his family's new house to be built on Maryland's Eastern Shore. A mock-up of the room was created for the National Symphony Orchestra's 1989 Decorators' Show House, and the room was recreated when Edward's parents built their house the next year. The bed has an exercise ring on the headboard (not attached when the photograph was taken) and side boards that can be raised so Edward will not fall out. A lift to raise the mattress to a sitting position was intended but was not installed because of difficulties with the manufacturer (Figure 1.1). A hydraulic lift, however, was installed in the changing table along the wall. Nancy, Edward's mother, finds the lift, adjacent sink, and drawers more of a convenience for her and pleasure for Edward than she had anticipated (Figure 1.2).

A built-in counter, with shelves and cabinets above, is angled and cantilevered so Edward can roll up in his wheelchair (Figure 1.3). Edward also likes to lie on the rug in front of the counter. The design of the oak furniture seamlessly combines the practical with the aesthetic.

Just inside the door to Edward's bedroom, a recess for a chest of drawers was built. Instead, a standing table in which Edward exercises his legs was installed. From there Edward talks to his mother, who watches him through the open door as she works in the kitchen (Figure 1.4). Between the standing table and changing table is the door to Edward's undecorated bathroom consisting of whirl-

FIGURE 1.1
Edward's bed with exercise bar (ring removed) and tape recorder on headstand.

FIGURE 1.2
Changing table, sink, and cabinets.

FIGURE 1.3
Wheelchair-accessible counter and shelves above. Edward's special tricycle is near the window.

FIGURE 1.4
Standing table is in an alcove near the bedroom door.

pool bath/shower, accessible sink, and toilet. There is room enough for a side transfer from wheelchair to toilet and if Edward is eventually able to transfer himself, bars will be mounted on the reinforced walls (Figure 1.5).

From his room, Edward wheels to the kitchen, where he can eat with his family at the dining table or have his own snack at the counter with a parent sitting next to him to assist (Figure 1.6). The passage from the bedroom to the kitchen is straight and wide, and from the kitchen it is a few feet to the garage, which is the only entrance with a ramp. Although all the rooms have 3-foot-wide openings and are accessible, Edward happily spends most of his time in his room or in the kitchen.

An intercom system links all the rooms and when Edward is lying in bed or sunning himself in the chair next to the bed, Nancy will, much to his delight, call him on the intercom to say "hi."

Nancy and her husband, Bill, included an elevator in their house in case Edward wanted to visit his siblings' or parents' second floor bedrooms. However, at the time of this writing, the family had been in the house nearly a year and the elevator had yet to be used. Nancy views that as "an unexpected bonus"—Edward is so happy in his new room that he does not need to be with his brothers and sisters constantly. This is not the only time Edward has delighted and surprised his parents with unanticipated skills and maturity—as when he mastered his special tricycle.

Ms. Iglesias gave the parents the decorated bedroom they wanted for Edward and more importantly she captured the certainty that his potential cannot be narrowly defined.

FIGURE 1.5
Toilet with wheelchair room to side.

FIGURE 1.6
Edward at lowered kitchen counter.

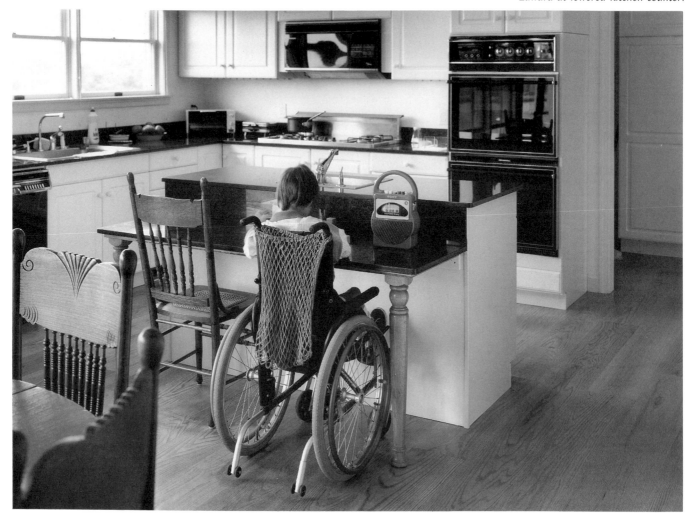

Chapter 2

A DOCTOR'S HOUSE

A slate walk leads from the driveway to the front doors. There are no steps; the walk slopes up noticeably. There is a low peephole in the left front door, and a small hook is screwed into the right door (Figure 2.1). The hook allows the owner to close the door behind him without having to turn his motorized wheelchair around toward the house to the reach the door lever. The double doors (each

FIGURE 2.1
Doctor's House—slate ramp and front doors.

panel wide enough for a wheelchair) open onto the main floor of the house, which consists of dining room, kitchen, bedrooms, family room, study, and elevator/stairs.

The bedrooms are at the right end of the house. The door to the son's room has been angled, and the master bedroom door opposite it has been widened to 36 inches. The angling and widening of doors provide easier wheelchair access (Figure 2.2).

All the electrical devices in the master bedroom can be controlled from a panel attached to the doctor's nightstand. And within easy reach on his nightstand are lamp, dictating machine, snacks, and a telephone with an adapted grip. Without the difficulty of getting out of bed, the doctor can adjust the temperature, operate the television, adjust the lights, or turn on a heating pad (Figure 2.3).

At the opposite end of the main floor, the doctor added a wing consisting of an elevator and wraparound stairs, adjacent study, and a family room behind the study (Figure 2.4). With a beveled threshold and doors that both open when the lever handle is pushed, access to the family room is convenient (Figure 2.5). Once in the room, the doctor rolls up to the drop leaf table, where he can lean his arm while facing guests seated around the perimeter (Figure 2.6).

FIGURE 2.2
Child's bedroom to right, master bedroom to left.

FIGURE 2.3
Control panel in master bedroom.

FIGURE 2.4
Tall windows (behind railing) light the elevator/stair atrium. The study is at far left.

FIGURE 2.5
Doors to family room.

FIGURE 2.6
Seating arrangement in family room.

To the left of the doors into the family room is a toggle switch for the elevator. Locating the switch there rather than next to the elevator allows the doctor to push the switch to open the elevator door and roll straight in (Figures 2.5 and 2.7). Had the switch been next to the elevator the doctor would have had to reposition himself after pressing the switch to either get out of the path of the door or to be at the right angle to enter the elevator. Not liking elevators, but needing one to get to lower level and backyard, the doctor specified an open elevator, with clear side walls and no ceiling. Skylights and windows drench the elevator, the stairs around the elevator, the elevator landing, and the adjacent study with abundant natural lighting, turning a necessity into a delight (Figure 2.7).

In the study, the chess table is set high and cantilevered to provide unobstructed access for the wheelchair. To the table's left is the control for the overhead fan (Figure 2.8). All electrical controls have been lowered and all electrical outlets have been raised. On the wall opposite the chess table is a cantilevered work desk and at the far end is a slanted newspaper reading stand, relieving the doctor of the strain of holding the paper. Inexpensive devices, such as the

FIGURE 2.7
*Elevator, stairs, study beyond, and elevator
toggle switch to right.*

FIGURE 2.8
*Chess table in the study. The elevator is
visible through the window.*

FIGURE 2.9
Desk and newspaper reading stand in the study.

headset, aid dexterity, and word processing macros make typing on the computer faster and easier (Figure 2.9).

In the other rooms on the main floor similar minor adjustments such as cantilevering the kitchen table, and, in the master bathroom, adding an accordion mirror and raising the floor assure accessibility.

The lower floor of the house, which has guest bedrooms and less formal rooms, is level with and provides access to the backyard.

Knowing precisely the extent of his mobility and dexterity limitations, conceiving of straightforward solutions, buying a house in which vertical circulation is secondary, and having the requisite finances, this suburban Washington, D.C. doctor subtly created accessibility—without an architect or interior designer and without the stigma associated with jarring modifications that shout "done for the disabled." In fact, the feature most associated with physical disability, the elevator atrium, is the house's most pleasing detail.

Chapter 3

NATIONAL ASSOCIATION OF HOME BUILDERS' DEMONSTRATION HOUSE

Dreams sell houses: prospective buyers want to hear about marble bathtubs and songbirds in the backyard, not about grab bars and fire sprinklers. But the National Association of Home Builders wants its members to address the realities of aging owners and possible fires in the dream houses they build.

The NAHB built such a house near Washington, D.C., and the siting and exterior treatment will not shatter the dreams of speculative home builders or prospective buyers. The land slopes up to the house so that a slight ramp runs along the front, concealed by a railing. An imperceptible 2 feet of height has been added to the garage door to accommodate a high van with a wheelchair lift (Figure 3.1). Inside the garage, a low ramp leads into the house.

FIGURE 3.1
National Association of Home Builders' house.

FIGURE 3.2
Dining room doors, deck, and backyard.

Around back, the dining room doors open onto the deck and the yard, without steps, because of the sloped landscaping (Figure 3.2).

The interior is open and bright in this approximately 2300-square-foot house, without any of the rooms being oversized. The corridors are 4 feet wide—all doorways have 3 foot openings—and the rooms have generous circulation paths or open central spaces. In the bathroom and den/guest room, with low pile carpeting suitable for a someone in a wheelchair, there is good clearance as the doors open onto wide passages (Figure 3.3). The interior layout has been subtly manipulated to provide excellent maneuvering room for someone using a walker or in a wheelchair (Figures 3.4 and 3.5).

Further accommodation for the person with a mobility or dexterity disability is apparent throughout. Door and window handles require little strength or agility to operate (Figures 3.6 and 3.3). The kitchen's low pullout drawers provide better work surfaces

FIGURE 3.3
Den/guest room with wide passage. Built-in wheelchair-height ironing board is on the opposite wall. The push-button door handles require little strength or agility to operate.

SECOND FLOOR

FIGURE 3.5
Second floor plan. (From National Association of Home Builders and Nantichoke Homes, Inc. Reproduced with permission of the NAHB.)

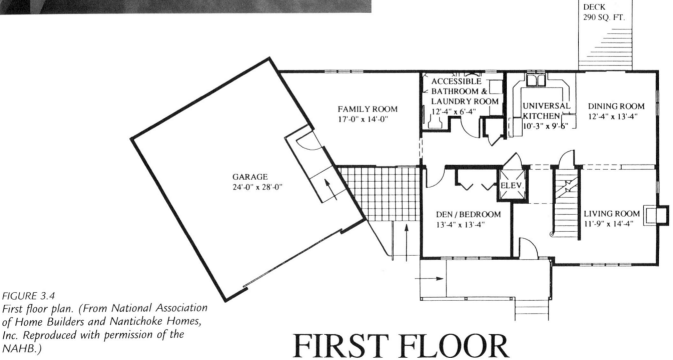

FIGURE 3.4
First floor plan. (From National Association of Home Builders and Nantichoke Homes, Inc. Reproduced with permission of the NAHB.)

FIRST FLOOR

FIGURE 3.6
Crank for controlling both window locks.

FIGURE 3.7
Kitchen.

than counter tops for someone in a wheelchair. Cooktop controls, placed at the front, can be adjusted without reaching over hot burners. The cabinets have large pulls. The upper group of cabinets can be lowered and the one beneath the sink can be removed for wheelchair clearance. Lazy susans, a pass through, and doors on the dining room as well as the kitchen side of the cabinets are added conveniences (Figure 3.7).

Accessible bathrooms have roll-in baths/showers with benches, grab bars, and an adjustable height shower head, which can also be held by hand (Figure 3.8). Painted and grooved plastic grab bars for the toilet—with enough space for diagonal transfer from a wheelchair—and a ceramic cover for the pipes under the sink remove the institutional look from an accessible bathroom (Figures

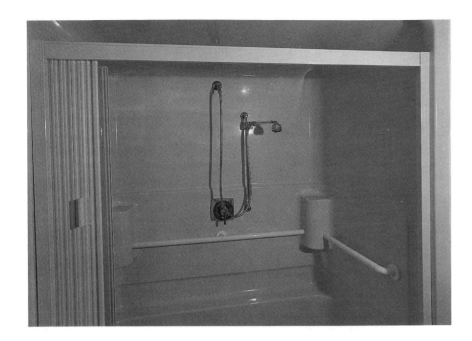

FIGURE 3.8
Roll-in shower.

FIGURE 3.9
Toilet with grab bars.

3.9 and 3.10). With the exception of the security panel and thermostat (an oversight), all electrical controls have been lowered and the outlets raised to better suit the possible range of sizes of occupants (Figure 3.11).

Special fire alarms were added for someone with communications disabilities. In case of fire, strobes flash and special wall recep-

FIGURE 3.10
Sink with lever handles and panel concealing pipes.

tacles in the den/guest room are activated. A fan, light, or bed vibrator plugged into these receptacles would activate during a fire. The fan and vibrator provide tactile alarms needed by someone who is visually as well as hearing impaired.

An elevator is included in the demonstration house, which exceeds the basic NAHB recommendation that closets be stacked so that they can be converted to an elevator shaft if needed at a later date. (All products were donated or provided at cost by the manufacturers. A list of products used is available from the National Association of Home Builders Research Center, 400 Prince George's Boulevard, Upper Marlboro, MD 20772-8731, [301] 249-4000, fax [301] 249-3096.)

Did the NAHB, with the endorsement of the U.S. Fire Administration and the U.S. Architectural and Transportation Barriers Compliance Board, add fire safety and accessibility without destroying the dream house? The purchase of the house will be the most convincing proof, but first the sluggish real estate market must improve. Until then, the best testaments are those of NAHB Research Center board member Barry Rosengarten and David Williamson, U.S. HUD senior executive, disability consultant to NAHB, and a user of a wheelchair. Rosengarten's new luxury housing development in New Jersey includes accessibility features used in the NAHB demonstration house. Williamson states categorically that "most of the special features incorporated here (the demonstration house) will be generally standard in houses of 2001."

FIGURE 3.11
Elevator, push button door handles, wide
doorways and corridors, and lowered light
and elevator controls.

Chapter 4

ACCESSIBLE APARTMENT BATHROOM

When Susan Dynes, architectural designer and historic preservationist, converted a small kitchen in her parents' apartment into an accessible bathroom she was both client and designer. The Dyneses live in one of Washington's grand old apartment buildings, designated a local landmark for its ornate and luxurious early twentieth-century facade and public spaces.

A rear bathroom in the apartment has a large, deep tub supported on claw legs. When Dynes moved back into her parents' apartment, she made that bathroom accessible to the degree possible by attaching a grab bar to the tub and adding several grab bars along the walls. But once it became too difficult for her to use the high bathtub, she decided that making a former kitchen for servants into a bathroom would give her better accessibility than any further changes possible in the existing bathroom. The bathrooms are opposite each other and equally convenient to her bedroom.

In the new bathroom (Figure 4.1), Susan can either sit in or stand when she showers. If she stands, she can use either the long vertical grab bars or the horizontal one that doubles as a shower curtain rod. Her contractor suggested making the curtain rod strong enough to be a grab bar. Another proposal by the contractor, to redo the floor, was not acceptable to Dynes as it would have altered the historic fabric of the apartment. As the shower floor is higher than the bathroom floor, a small ramp goes from the original tile floor to the sill of the shower.

FIGURE 4.1
Susan Dynes's bathroom was originally a kitchen. Note the good wheelchair turning space in the bathroom, knee space at the sink, slight ramp to the shower, which has both horizontal and vertical grab bars. Toilet is at far right.

FIGURE 4.2
Toilet in Susan Dynes's bathroom has angled grab bars close by, and vertical and horizontal bars on the wall to the right.

The toilet next to the shower stall might seem tight (Figure 4.2), but its position along with the angled grab bars to either side, provide the support she needs to transfer.

For the sink, the contractor suggested, and Susan agreed to, a Corian counter top, which might seem extravagant but works well for a cantilevered span. Susan created a functional sink area with wide knee space, a faucet that can be raised up for washing her hair, good lighting, and convenient counter space.

Dyne's bathroom reflects her needs and the limitations of the space she had to work in. By putting toilet, shower, and sink adjacent to each other, she freed up the requisite turning space for a wheelchair, but also created an unusual layout. In addition, Susan used more grab bars and positioned them differently from those in other accessible bathrooms. Most accessible toilets stalls are designed wide enough for side, or at least diagonal, transfer from a wheelchair, with horizontal grab bars along the wall. For Susan, angled grab bars close to the seat better met her needs. (Some people who use walkers also want the grab bars closer to the seat in public bathrooms.) Sometimes the standards for accessible bathrooms most be varied to serve a particular person's strengths and weaknesses and to fit the available space. But few clients have the design skills to specify the details or have a contractor who is able to make good suggestions for improved accessibility.

Chapter 5

ACCESSIBLE PATHS

The child is less than 10 years old, weighs less than 40 pounds, and uses a wheelchair always pushed by an adult. As the child is easily carried within the house, either between rooms or between floors, making the grounds accessible had higher priority than making the house accessible. Two families—only a few blocks apart in the upper northwest Washington, D.C. area, but with very different financial resources and houses—each wanted to provide accessible paths on which to push their child's wheelchair, while creating aesthetically pleasing landscapes.

The more modest house's only path from the driveway to the house was up a run of steps up a low hill. From the street, there was a curb, path, and step to the front door. In the backyard, at the far corner, was a swing with a special seat and straps to securely hold the young girl; but the route to the swing was over cracked, uneven asphalt and dirt.

John Lemieux of A. W. Landscapes regraded the front yard and created two new paths of large stone slabs, with the gray blue blocks set close together. A level path leads from a slight ramp at the curb to the step at the front door, while the second path curves from the widened driveway past a new terrace with seating area up to the front door. Widening the driveway provides more room for getting the girl in and out of the family van and for maneuvering her wheelchair. It also meant there was space to store garbage cans (Figure 5.1).

In the backyard, the swing occupies its original position, but a level stone patio has been put down and the ground under the swing has a more attractive mulch covering (Figure 5.2). It is still a step up from the backyard to the back door.

At the more architecturally impressive house, the path from the driveway and sidewalk led to two steps up to an understated front porch. At the back of the house, the rear porch was a step lower than the house and the ground was a step lower than the porch.

FIGURE 5.1
Front yard of the more modest house with
paths from street to house and from
driveway to house.

FIGURE 5.2
Rear yard of more modest house, with stone
terrace leading to child's swing having
replaced uneven, unsightly asphalt and dirt
surface.

Architect Edward Wykoff designed a wider, deeper, more prepossessing front porch with substantial squat columns, and he eliminated the step at the front door. Landscape architect Lawrence V. Frank, ASLA, replaced the old path with a curved, gently rising brick one to the front porch (Figure 5.3). Subsequently, after Wykoff had left the Washington area, the owners hired architect David Jones to redesign the rear porch structure as a formal, columned first floor family room, with a master bedroom above. As this rear structure is now level with the rest of the house, the change in level from house to rear structure is gone. The step from the rear to the ground was also eliminated in Frank's re-landscaping of the backyard with a brick path. The path curves eloquently to a settee at the edge of the property and then continues to curve gently down to a large circular terrace (Figures 5.4 and 5.5). From the terrace, level ground leads to a gate and driveway. As it is a double gate, it can be opened wide enough to accommodate a person in a wheelchair.

The owners of the larger house, having first done the front yard landscaping, added an elevator when the rear structure and rear yard were redesigned. And in the master bedroom's bath, next to the tub, is a low counter where they can dry their son after his bath. The owners of the more modest house also plan to add an elevator or if that proves too difficult, move to a house that can more easily be made accessible.

FIGURE 5.3
Front yard of the larger house, with paths from driveway and street to new front porch flush with front door sill.

FIGURE 5.4
Rear yard of the larger house, looking from the back door toward the lower terrace. The sill of the back door is flush with the brick path.

By dealing with landscaping before the interiors, both families addressed first the place where lack of accessibility created the greater, immediate burden—pushing the wheelchair between the van or car and house. Lawrence Frank kept his paths as gentle as possible, less than an 8 degree incline, whereas Lemieux had less space, so his path from the driveway is steeper. The steepness of the path was not a serious factor for either family, as they always push the wheelchair. Furthermore, the owners of the more modest home did not eliminate the steps at the doors because they do not think it will ever be a real burden to raise or lower the wheelchair over them. Only as the child grew older did the eventuality of carrying an older, heavier child up and down stairs become a concern and lead to interior redesign to improve accessibility.

FIGURE 5.5
*Rear yard of the larger house, looking from
the lower terrace toward the house.*

Both families succeed in creating quite attractive landscapes suited to their particular aesthetics and accessibility criteria. Yet the paths are not wheelchair ramps. They are not designed to meet accessibility codes, and they do not make the grounds or house look as if they were designed for someone in a wheelchair.

Section III

SCHOOLS

The institutions described in this section form an impressive group. Two were recently profiled in *Life* magazine; one was described 150 years earlier by Charles Dickens. Another is the only school of its kind in the world. Two are named after pioneering American women, and three are tributes to American philanthropy. The newest school is less than 2 years old, the oldest closer to 200 years. Collectively, they educate, train, and rehabilitate people as young as elementary school age and as old as senior citizens, with a wide range of disabilities.

Yet, to the expert on low vision who lived in two institutions for the blind and to the parent who has to fight to get a child with a mobility disability into the neighborhood school, most of these educational facilities are not good selections. It would be far better, in their opinion, to profile primary schools, high schools, and colleges designed to educate the general population and accessible to all—that is, schools that meet the letter and the spirit of federal laws dating back 25 years. It is debatable, however, whether many schools meet the letter, let alone the spirit, of federal accessibility and mainstreaming laws.

Mainstreaming (educating children with physical, psychological, learning, or developmental disabilities in classes and schools with nondisabled students), like all issues relating to accessibility, is complex and controversial. What constitutes legally sufficient mainstreaming and deciding whether mainstreaming is the best solution for all children are unresolved questions, beyond the scope of this book. But it is safe to assume that under the added impetus of the ADA, mainstreaming will become much more widespread, the general schools will be nearly as accessible as the special schools, and the special schools will continue to exist.

To find good educational models of accessibility, it is therefore necessary to look almost entirely to schools that already serve, in significant numbers, children and adults with disabilities. These institutions have thought out the accessibility needs of students with disabilities and made the requisite physical accommodations.

These schools are relatively specialized, educating children and some adults with one or perhaps two disabilities. Therefore, they tailor their accessibility to suit their particular constituency rather than trying to be equally accessible to all of the disabled population. The Columbia Lighthouse and the Helen Keller National Center, for example, use tactile warnings and other similar devices to assure accessibility for the visually impaired and blind. (At Helen Keller, the students are visually impaired or blind and also hearing impaired or deaf.) But neither institution is especially accessible for someone who has a mobility impairment. The Henry Viscardi High School, on the other hand, is especially suited for children who are in wheelchairs or without some limbs, but it is not especially accessible for students who are visually or hearing impaired. Gallaudet's strength is in educating and being accessible for people who are hearing impaired or deaf. But just as Gallaudet has some students who are hearing impaired and also visually impaired or in wheelchairs, the other institutions have some students with multiple disabilities. They accommodate people with various disabilities, but still remain more accessible for people with one specific type of disability.

The Resnik School, although primarily serving a nondisabled student body, emphasizes mobility accessibility. Of the several features aiding mobility, the most significant are the multipurpose room with ramps and stairs leading up to the stage and that the school is a one-story building with a simple layout and a symbolic focus. That all students enter the stage from the front is as strong a statement of equal access that an architect can make. (See Chapter 20 for a stage without steps.) Resnik's straightforward plan can also be more easily comprehended by and is, therefore, more accessible to students who are developmentally, learning, or visually disabled. Architects have a more positive role to play than simply eliminating physical barriers and accommodating nonarchitectural accessibility features in school (and other) buildings, although neither function has probably been sufficiently appreciated by architects. They can design buildings (preferably one story) like the Resnik and Viscardi Schools that have strong spatial organization and a symbolic focus. (See Chapter 19 on Chinn Aquatic & Fitness Center.) A well-designed environment is physically, mentally, and psychologically accessible and encourages all students—disabled and nondisabled—to believe in their potential.

Chapter 6

GALLAUDET UNIVERSITY

Gallaudet claims to be the world's only liberal arts university for the deaf. But it was the successful revolt in March 1988 by students, staff, and faculty against the appointment of a hearing person as president that brought the school international publicity. The Gallaudet trustees' initial rejection as president of an academician who is deaf parallels American society's limited efforts—until recently—to address the communication needs of people who are deaf or have impaired hearing or speech.

In 1864, Abraham Lincoln signed a charter authorizing Gallaudet to award college degrees. A few years later, Frederick Withers, Frederick Law Olmsted, and Calvert Vaux designed for the school, in northeast Washington, D.C., a distinguished complex of collegiate gothic architecture. These academic and residential buildings are linked by wide pedestrian paths to the school's more mundane twentieth-century buildings. The wide paths are not only aesthetically pleasing, but—according to campus architect Michael Fields, AIA, who is deaf—provide the necessary space for people communicating primarily through sign language. (Figure 6.1)

When personal communication is not possible, Gallaudet employs visual and other nonaudio communication devices.* At the entrance to dorms (Figure 6.2), a wheelchair-accessible emergency button summons help without voice communications. (By comparison, another Washington, D.C. university still installs emergency boxes that require voice communications and are too tall for someone in a wheelchair.) Gallaudet's elevator emergency buttons do not require voice communications either; when the button is pressed, a "help is on the way" sign is illuminated, and the campus police are notified. Flashing yellow beacons along a building's roof line and inside signal that the building's fire alarm has been sounded.

*Background noise is very disturbing for people using hearing aids, so Gallaudet uses extra soundproofing in its buildings.

FIGURE 6.1
Wide pedestrian path providing necessary space for people signing.

FIGURE 6.2
Emergency button at dormitory entrance. No speech is required.

In nonemergency situations, flashing beacons and blinking lights are also used extensively to get the attention of people who are unaware of audible signals. When someone leaves the library through an emergency door or with a book not checked out, a beacon lights at the checkout desk. In the gym, a flashing beacon means the referee called a foul. When a computer beeps to indicate that operator action is required, a light bulb next to the keyboard goes on. In offices and dorm rooms, a light bulb blinks when the doorbell has been pressed. In the dorm rooms for students who are visually and hearing impaired, a fan turns on when the doorbell is rung. (Gallaudet also has lowered peepholes in dormitory doors for students in wheelchairs, and the university provides tactile maps of the campus for students who are blind.) When a text telephone has an incoming call, an overhead desk lamp blinks.

The text telephone is the most immediate, most efficient communications device for people with hearing or speech impairments. Seen throughout Gallaudet, the text telephone is either mounted below a pay telephone or adjacent to a desk phone. The user types a message in and waits for a reply, each displayed in order on a small one-line monitor. Some text telephones also provide a printout of the conversation.

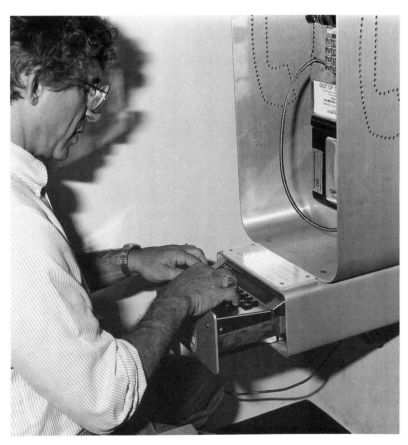

FIGURE 6.3
Michael Fields, AIA, typing on text telephone attached to a pay phone.

FIGURE 6.4
Pay telephone at dormitory is positioned so that user has privacy. Notice symbol of text telephone.

Text telephones are slower than voice phones noted Gallaudet architect Michael Fields, and users do not want passersby eavesdropping by reading the monitors. Therefore, Gallaudet provides a chair at each pay telephone, positioned to assure privacy (Figures 6.3, 6.4). Unlike the text telephone, other common text displayers such as captioned televisions, vibrating beepers (carried by the Gallaudet maintenance workers), one-line electronic message displays, and large video display monitors (used at Baltimor–Washington International Airport to page passengers and provide other information) are limited to one-way communications. The paramount importance of the text telephone is acknowledged by Title IV of the Americans with Disabilities Act, which required that, by July 26, 1993, telephone companies relay messages between voice and text telephones; for the first time, direct communications between a person with a speech or hearing impairment using a text telephone and another person using a voice telephone is possible.

Many of the communication devices used at Gallaudet are also used in the home. At Michael Fields's house, for example, the front and back doorbells, burglar/fire alarm, text telephone, and baby monitor are wired to the lights. The number and duration of blinking lights indicate which device has been triggered.

The communication devices at Gallaudet are becoming increasingly common at other public and commercial buildings. Newer hotels have visual fire alarms and adjustable volume telephones and some federal buildings and airports have text telephones. "ADA Accessibility Guidelines for Buildings and Facilities," prepared by the U.S. Architectural and Transportation Barriers Compliance Board, specifies visual fire alarms, nonverbal emergency systems in elevators as well as visual and audible elevator floor signals and adjustable volume telephones and text telephones (without mentioning the need for privacy and a seat) for those buildings covered by the Americans with Disabilities Act.

The rallying cry of Gallaudet University's charismatic president, I. King Jordan, is "The deaf can do . . . anything." The ADA assures them that they will have the necessary means of communication. Architects and designers will need to ensure that the best environment for effective communication by people with hearing or speech impairments is created.

Chapter 7

JUDITH A. RESNIK ELEMENTARY SCHOOL

Thomas Clark, AIA, was exasperated with his visitor as the two of them toured the new Montgomery County (MD) elementary school he had designed. Clark, who has been honored by architectural and educational groups for his school designs, tried to discuss architecture and spatial organization, while the visitor focused on curb cuts and door widths. But both perspectives are valid, as the Judith A. Resnik School, named after one of the seven astronauts killed in the *Challenger* explosion, is a cornerstone in the county's efforts to mainstream children with disabilities into schools with nondisabled students.

A suburb of Washington, D.C., Montgomery is one of the nation's wealthiest counties. Its northern tip is still rural and agricultural, but housing and commercial buildings are rapidly displacing the farms. The residential southern end of the county is populated largely by people who work for the federal government and those who have grown wealthy from lobbying it. Many families move to the county for its renowned public schools.

The Resnik School is one of the county's two schools for mainstreaming students with disabilities whose needs, in the opinion of the school administration, cannot be met at their neighborhood schools. Resnik has physical and occupational therapy rooms, an enlarged health unit with showers, changing rooms, and accessibility, which the neighborhood schools lack. Key to Resnik's accessibility is its one-story plan and level siting. Outside paths and corridors within the school are on grade without inclines, stairs, or elevator. Of the 600 students at Resnik, 40 are "physically challenged" (the school's term). The degree of mainstreaming for these 40 students depends on the individual student's abilities—some are in classes with the nondisabled; others are in special classes but have recess and lunch with the nondisabled students. Further integration throughout the school system is projected as new and renovated schools are made more accessible.

Montgomery County Public Schools' mainstreaming efforts are mandated by federal law. The Education of the Handicapped Act of 1975, amended and renamed in 1991 as the Individuals with Disabilities Education Act, requires children with disabilities to be educated in "the least restrictive setting," meaning an integrated social and educational environment. Under the 1975 Education Act, the Rehabilitation Act of 1973, and Title II of the Americans with Disabilities Act of 1990, the state and local school systems, as recipients of federal grants, have to integrate students with disabilities into the general school population. Maryland and Montgomery County have each prepared annual plans for mainstreaming children with disabilities, and the Montgomery County plan is still evolving in terms of the specifics of physical accessibility.

FIGURE 7.1
Plan of Judith A. Resnik Elementary School. (From Thomas Clark Associates Architects. Reproduced with permission of Thomas Clark Associates, Architects.)

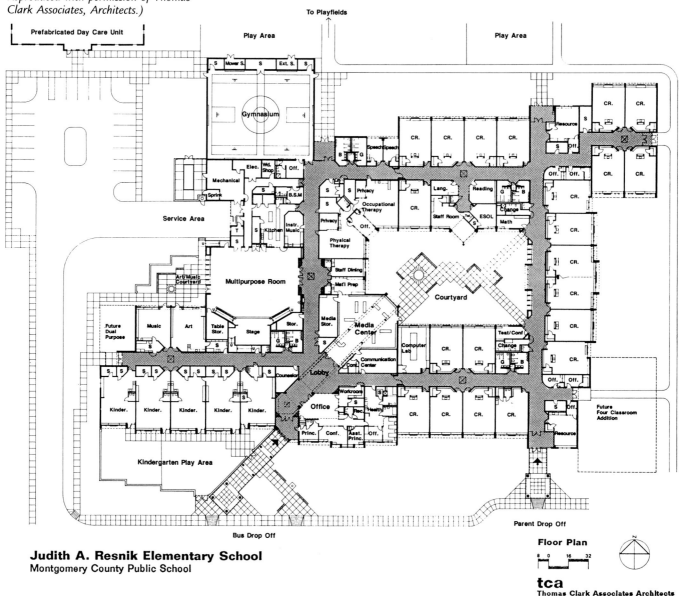

Judith A. Resnik Elementary School
Montgomery County Public School

Floor Plan

tca
Thomas Clark Associates Architects

To meet the varied educational, social, and physical needs of a mixed student body, Thomas Clark organized the Judith A. Resnik Elementary School, which opened in September 1991, around a courtyard, with the media center as the symbol of the school (Figure 7.1). Topped with a gabled roof soaring above the rest of the school and located at the end of the entrance lobby and at the corner of the courtyard, the media center is indeed the school's visual focus. The center has displaced the school office, traditionally given a prominent location, to the side of the entrance lobby (Figure 7.2). Clark has shifted the emphasis from administration to education—at least architecturally.

The media center, like all rooms in the school, is accessible for students in wheelchairs or using walking aids. Not only are doors wide, but many doorways are angled, requiring less maneuvering by someone in a wheelchair. In the classrooms, the sinks have padded pipes, knee space for wheelchairs, and the unusual feature of faucet handles mounted on the side rather than the rear, providing easier access. Unlike classrooms in other schools, the furniture is not crowded together, providing clearance for students using wheelchairs or other walking devices. Also, there are holders for crutches and—for some students—special seats that help them strengthen their muscles while in class (Figure 7.3). Of course, the bathrooms are accessible (i.e., wide passageway, grab bars, wide stalls, sinks at the right height with knee space, and properly placed mirrors, towels, and soap dispensers). The corridors are wide and have grab bars, and the water cooler has knee space and is recessed so as not to be an obstacle to someone who is visually impaired. (However, if the water cooler were in a wider recess, it would easier to approach in a wheelchair, see Figure 7.2.)

FIGURE 7.2
Looking south toward office. To the immediate right is the doorway to the multipurpose room, farther down the corridor is the water cooler.

The media center is the intended symbol of the Resnik School, but the multipurpose room (an auditorium/cafeteria) is the symbol of the school's accessibility (Figure 7.4). Rather than just steps up to the stage, Clark included two ramps. All students, disabled and nondisabled, are able to enter and exit the multipurpose room's stage from the front because there are stairs and ramps in front. No longer does the student with a disability suffer the indignity of using the ramp intended for moving props at the rear of the stage.

At the Resnik School, Thomas Clark demonstrated that accessibility can be mainstreamed into architecture successfully and subtly.

FIGURE 7.3
Classroom showing accessible sink. Behind the partition are clothes and wheelchair storage. At the left of the photograph are crutch holder and special seat.

FIGURE 7.4
Stage of multipurpose room, with ramps and stairs in front.

Chapter 8

HENRY VISCARDI HIGH SCHOOL

Forty years ago, Dr. Henry Viscardi, who was born without legs, started an employment service for the disabled at Albertson, Long Island that has grown into a nationally renowned educational, training, and employment program. The National Center for Disability Services' Henry Viscardi High School is, according to principal Joseph Russo, the only high school in the United States for students who are physically disabled and academically able. Seventy percent of its students go on to college, which is greater than the national average for all high school graduates. The Viscardi High School is a model of accessibility for students in wheelchairs or using walker or crutches.

Architect Angelo Francis Corva, AIA, designed the new Viscardi school, which opened in April 1989 as a largely self-contained one-story structure attached by a narrow corridor to the National Center for Disability Services (NCDS) building (Figure 8.1). Between the NCDS building and the high school is a courtyard enlivened with plantings and oxidized metal sculptures and enclosed by a large glass wall at the east end. This segmental arched glass expanse, the focus of the angled main corridor running from the high school entrance to the courtyard, faces two walls of student lockers (not visible in the photograph) (Figure 8.2). Stacked at two heights, some lockers have been modified by adding knobs on the outside and/or by placing extra shelves inside for students whose reach falls between the lower and upper lockers.

Beyond the locker or common area is a lobby with recessed entrances to the student bathrooms. As each one has separate in and out doors, students only have to push them open, which is easier than pulling, and they do not open into a passerby. These lightweight doors have hinges requiring minimal pressure and are self-closing (Figure 8.3). In the bathrooms, the roll-in showers have high and low clothes hooks. (Seldom do accessible bathrooms in other facilities have a hook at a suitable height for someone in a

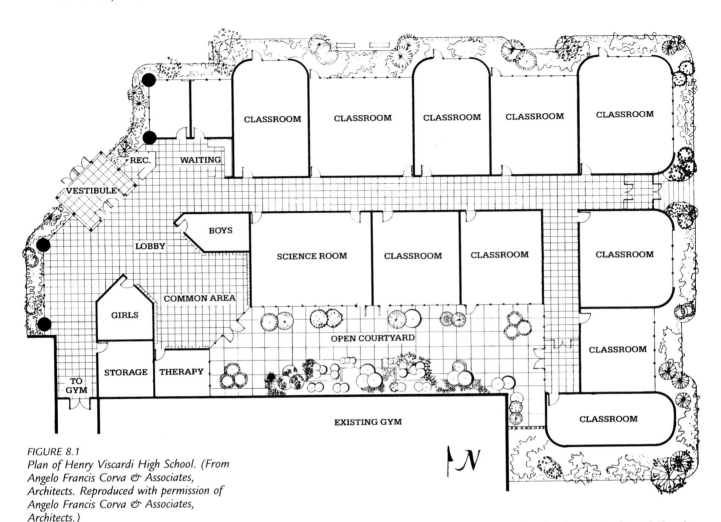

FIGURE 8.1
Plan of Henry Viscardi High School. (From Angelo Francis Corva & Associates, Architects. Reproduced with permission of Angelo Francis Corva & Associates, Architects.)

wheelchair.) Floor-mounted grab bars flank the urinals, while the toilets have fixed grab bars to the side and rear with an additional movable bar on the side (Figures 8.4 and 8.5). Allowing for the different clearances required by different heights of wheelchairs, the bathroom sinks are at two heights, with the waste pipes recessed to protect the knees of someone in a wheelchair. Large mirrors (one angled out at the top so that a person in a wheelchair looking up at the mirror sees his or her image rather than the wall opposite), cup dispenser and paper dispenser/trash receptacle are positioned for users in wheelchairs (Figure 8.6). Automatic sensors control the faucets, urinals, and toilets.

Adjacent to the girls' bathroom are two accessible drinking fountains at different heights and a drinking-cup dispenser for those unable to or preferring not to drink from the spout (Figure 8.7). (In other facilities, placing cup dispensers next to inaccessible drinking fountains and in bathrooms might be an acceptable alternative to adding accessible drinking fountains.) In Figure 8.2, notice that the trash can blocks a side approach to the drinking fountain and cup dispenser. In many buildings, accessible features are rendered inaccessible by thoughtlessly placed obstacles such as maintenance supplies or bicycles chained to railings.

FIGURE 8.2
Looking from the lobby toward the common
area and courtyard on other side of the
glass wall.

FIGURE 8.3
In and out doors to boys' bathroom.

FIGURE 8.4
Urinals with grab bars.

FIGURE 8.5
Toilet with two fixed and one movable
grab bar.

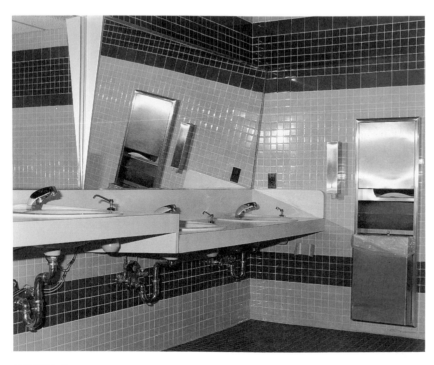

FIGURE 8.6
Bathroom sink, mirrors, cup dispenser, and
trash receptacle.

FIGURE 8.7
Accessible drinking fountains at two heights
and cup dispenser.

In the Henry Viscardi High School classrooms, which have the same hinged doors as the bathrooms, the height and angle of the tables can be adjusted to suit students in wheelchairs (Figure 8.8). At the science work station, knee space for someone in a wheelchair runs the entire length of the table, and its height can be raised for someone using a taller, motorized wheelchair. (Figure 8.9)

FIGURE 8.8
Adjustable classroom table.

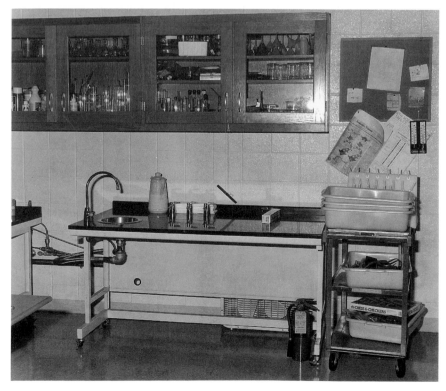

FIGURE 8.9
Science work station with wheelchair clearance.

In comparing the new high school building to the school's old quarters on the second floor of the National Center for Disability Services building (which has elevators), Joseph Russo said the students find the new wide corridors easier to negotiate and that everyone preferred the new light, bright atmosphere created by the large expanses of glass and skylights. Russo then elaborated on the details he considered most important: the adjustable furniture in the classrooms, the common area near the courtyard (where boyfriend and girlfriend, like teenagers in any high school, can linger until told to go to class), and the bathroom sensors. The automatic controls enable students who previously needed assistance to use the bathroom by themselves. Russo commented how difficult adolescence is for any child and how much harder it is for a child with a disability who needs help in the bathroom. Accessibility improves one's psychological as well as physical well-being.

Chapter 9

SCHOOLS FOR PEOPLE WITH VISUAL DISABILITIES

The accessibility guidelines accompanying the Americans with Disabilities Act have limited but quite detailed recommendations to improve accessibility for people with visual impairments. The guidelines eliminate certain architectural barriers, establish warnings for unavoidable hazards, and specify signs that will help orient the visually impaired. To understand the visual accessibility issues not yet addressed by or beyond the scope of the ADA guidelines, it is best to look to the schools and institutions serving people with vision disabilities.

"Visually impaired" is not a euphemism for "blind"; the majority of visually impaired people have at least some sight. Only 10 percent of the visually impaired population reads braille. The ADA guidelines, therefore, require both braille and raised print signs and emphasize low-glare, high-contrast signs with large print that can be read by many visually impaired people. Some vision experts, however, argue against including braille on signs, in view of the low percentage of braille users.

Some visually impaired people rely on companions to get about, whereas others use service dogs or canes. People who carry canes have different preferences as to their length and the method of using them. Furthermore, some use the cane one way in a familiar environment and differently in a new setting. A person who is hearing impaired as well as visually impaired cannot hear the sound cues that a visually impaired person depends on, for example, in an elevator or crossing the street. In designing better accessibility for people who are visually impaired, the range of their visual acuity and their varied travel techniques must be considered; no single design solution will serve every visually impaired person's needs.

The Royal National Institute for the Blind (London) has identified four principles in designing for the person with a visual disability:

- Use sound cues to orient the "totally blind person."
- Have texture contrasts on floors and walls for orientation.
- Provide good lighting, since the majority of visually impaired people have some sight.
- Create color contrast to make objects and furnishings more distinguishable.

Other experts on mobility for the visually impaired also recommend that furniture that is low or has sharp edges should not be used, that plants should not be in the walkways (a frequent restaurant motif), that the projection or overhang of immovable objects be limited, and that color and tactile contrasts be used to warn of hazards as well as to aid in orientation. Above all else, buildings should have simple spatial organizations that are easy to comprehend and move through.

Outside the Perkins School for the Blind in Watertown, MA, probably the oldest such institution in the United States, the students know it is safe to cross the street when the chimes sound,

FIGURE 9.1
Outdoor tactile model of the grounds of the Perkins School for the Blind.

signaling a red light for the cars. On the Perkins grounds, a tactile model of the school's Elysian collegiate gothic campus once helped students form a mental image of the campus and the relationship between buildings and topography. The model is no longer used, because it does not include recent buildings (Figure 9.1). Not far from the model is the track, where each runner stays in his or her lane by holding onto a ring on a guide wire next to the lane (Figure 9.2). Distance runners who are visually impaired hold onto a short string carried by a fellow runner. At Perkins and a nearby munitions factory converted to a shopping mall, the nosing of stairs is painted in a high contrast color, making it more visible and less of a hazard to visually as well as nonvisually impaired people.

When Charles Dickens traveled to the United States in 1842, he visited Perkins and wrote at length about Laura Bridgman, the school's first deaf and blind student to be educated. Dickens's account in *American Notes* led Helen Keller's parents, 40 years later, to hire a graduate of Perkins, Anne Sullivan, to teach their deaf and blind daughter. Keller (1880–1968) would later travel with Anne

FIGURE 9.2
Perkins School track with guide wires and rings.

Sullivan from her home in Alabama to study at Perkins. She went on to graduate with honors from Radcliffe College, and, in the opinion of historian Arthur Schlesinger, "perhaps more than any other single person she had shown the world the human potential of the blind."

Three years before Keller's death, in 1965, the Helen Keller National Center for Deaf-Blind Youths and Adults was established on Long Island's bucolic North Shore. In the center's administration building, each corridor has a different color and texture walls to help orient students and staff. Since a stairwell is dangerous if unexpected, the walls flanking the door to the stairs are faced in brick. The distinctive change in wall texture warns people that the door opens into stairs. Any blind person wishing to use the stairs can hold onto the handrail that extends from the stairs around the landing, giving uninterrupted orientation in the stairwell (Figure 9.3). The two-story building also has an elevator, but since the users cannot hear or see when the cab reaches their destination, each passenger holds onto his or her own call button, which pops out when the desired floor is reached (Figure 9.4). Reminiscent of Perkins's running track with guide wires, the Helen Keller National Center's gym floor slopes upward near the walls to warn the athletes (Figure 9.5).

Although it lacks the pastoral charms of Perkins or the Keller Center, the Columbia Lighthouse for the Blind in downtown

FIGURE 9.3
Stairwell with continuous handrail, Helen Keller National Center.

FIGURE 9.4
Individual call buttons in an elevator, Helen Keller Center.

FIGURE 9.5
The gym floor slopes up to the wall, Helen Keller Center.

Washington, D.C. has a model office to train people with visual impairments for computer rather than manual labor employment. At the Lighthouse, doors to hazardous areas such as the telephone closet have scored knobs to indicate danger (Figure 9.6). Another tactile indicator, the change from bare floor to carpet a few feet east of the second-floor elevator landing, helps orient people. They memorize how many feet it is from the beginning of the carpet to specific offices (Figure 9.7). Computers enable more visually impaired people (and those with other disabilities) to work in offices, but little has yet been done to make the office environments more accessible for them. (For more on the office environment, see Section VI on computers/assistive technology and the United States Equal Employment Opportunities Commission.)

To help visually impaired clients comprehend the layout of the Maryland Rehabilitation Center in Baltimore, architectural model-builder Street Thoma and rehabilitation specialist Kurt Milam, who is blind, built a scaled, three-dimensional tactile model showing the building's corridors and offices (Figure 9.8). Thoma and

FIGURE 9.6
Scored doorknob at Columbia Lighthouse for the Blind.

FIGURE 9.7
Thaddeus Neumann, Columbia Lighthouse computer instructor, at carpet edge.

Milam had intended to paint the model's corridors the same colors as the building's, but were advised by experts on vision impairment to paint the model black on a yellow background, creating a high-contrast scene more legible for the visually impaired. Despite its usefulness, however, Carol Lewis, a counselor at the center, sees three limitations with such tactile models. Someone cannot comprehend the space solely from studying the model; he or she must also walk the corridors. If the viewer cannot see well enough to read the labels and does not know braille, then he or she cannot use the map to locate specific spaces. Lewis suggests audio cues to supplement the labels. Finally, a person who is visually impaired might not know the model exists. Baltimore's Fort McHenry, for example, contains a model of the facility, but Lewis, who is blind, went there for several years before anyone pointed the model out to her. A regularly repeated audio announcement would inform visitors who are visually impaired of the existence and location of the model. Lewis also favors audio announcements rather than audio cues in elevators so that she would not have to concentrate on counting the number of cues to know when she reaches her floor. If the floor numbers were announced, she could, like the other passengers, carry on a conversation. Despite their usefulness and obvious appeal to the visually impaired as well as the nonvisually impaired, tactile models need to be supplemented with audio communication.

When Professor Wolfgang Preiser tested tactile maps on visually impaired and nonvisually impaired students at the University

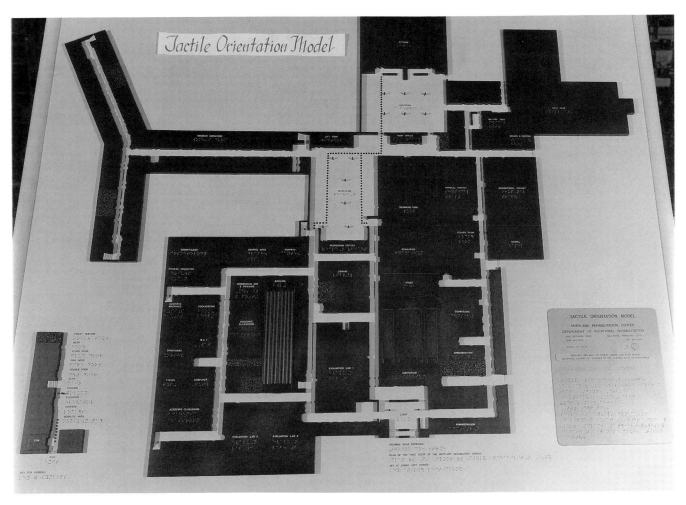

FIGURE 9.8
Maryland Rehabilitation Center's scaled tactile model of corridors and offices. (Model copyrighted by Street Thoma and Kurt Milam. Reproduced with permission of Street Thoma.)

of New Mexico, he found that tactile maps, like tactile models, need to be augmented. Using tactile maps alone the students took an unacceptably long time, in Preiser's opinion, to find their way around the campus. Professors Preiser and James G. Small subsequently combined the tactile maps with an audio system. Along a path that went through two university buildings and for approximately 600 m outside, a buried audio loop transmitted a signal to a special cane when the cane's tip was within 20–40 cm of the loop. The signal was converted to a vibration felt in the handle of the cane. The path of the audio loop was delineated on the tactile map. Professor Preiser also envisioned adding audio announcements at critical points along the path, such as emergency exits or stairs. In *Proceedings of the International Conference on Building Use and Safety Technology*, Preiser wrote that the system helps to

> improve orientation, direction finding, and mobility of visually impaired persons in buildings and public spaces where travel is difficult. This pertains to wide-open, undefined spaces, multi-level spaces, and curved or angled pathways without "shorelines," i.e., orienting aids such as bor-

ders, lines in pavements, etc. Traveling problems encountered by the visually impaired are caused in part by contemporary architecture, relating to such trends as open-plan schools and offices, or angular grids in the design of plazas and walkways.

Kevin Lynch, in his seminal *The Image of the City*, wrote that "the need to recognize and pattern our surroundings is so crucial and has such long roots in the past, that this image has wide practical and emotional importance to the individual. . . . A good environmental image gives its possessor an important sense of emotional security." And Lynch was writing about people with 20/20 vision. Buildings and spaces designed to be comprehensible to and, therefore, more easily traveled by the visually impaired will better serve, in a variety of ways, all users.

Section IV

MEDICAL FACILITIES

Chapter 10

NATIONAL REHABILITATION HOSPITAL AND THE WASHINGTON HOME AND HOSPICE

The 5-year-old National Rehabilitation Hospital (NRH) and the 103-year-old Washington Home and Hospice are architecturally very different. The hard glazed brick and metal sheathed columns of NRH evoke the high-tech look of the Bauhaus and J. J. Oud's architecture in the 1920s and early 1930s, while the warm brick tones and an occasional arched window of the Washington Home and Hospice suggest the comforting American domestic architecture of the late nineteenth century. The National Rehabilitation Hospital provides its outpatients and 160 inpatients with physical/occupational therapies and training to enable them to resume their lifestyle. The 189 bed Washington Home and Hospice is a permanent facility for patients who can no longer care for themselves. Despite differences of architectural style, population, and treatment goals, both medical facilities are designed to maintain the client's independence and dignity.

"Patients need to have the run of this place, to know it was built for them" was NRH President and Chief Executive Officer Edward Eckenhoff's charge to his architect, Ted Mariani, FAIA. Eckenhoff was speaking from the perspective of a hospital administrator who has "been disabled for the last 25 years." Not only did Eckenhoff act as Mariani's disabilities consultant on the project, but he had nurses, doctors, therapists, other medical staff, and disability advocacy groups talk to Mariani during the 2-year planning period. Eckenhoff said "I will always thank Ted for listening to the pros—to those who care for the disabled." Mariani used the ideal process: the consultants were involved early on and often had personal as well as professional expertise. (That several medical and nonmedical staff use wheelchairs probably also encourages patients in their own rehabilitation.)

Eckenhoff's radical vision that the hospital be designed for the convenience of the patient rather than the staff produced a building with seamless, complete accessibility. The main entrance, and the doors on each elevation are on grade. As in most medical facilities, the main door is automatic, but here the canopy in front extends to the adjacent parking garage (Figure 10.1). The people discharged at the entrance and those who move slowly up from the garage are protected from the weather. Once inside the hospital, a person in a wheelchair sees that everything from the reception desk to the cashier's counter is at his or her height rather than a standing person's height (Figure 10.2). One floor up, the public space has tables suspended from the ceiling, eliminating legs and bases, which are obstacles to people in wheelchairs. When the tables are not needed, they can be raised to the ceiling, freeing up the space for physical rehabilitation classes (Figure 10.3). The hospital's accommodation for people in wheelchairs extends to the patient's room, where the usually troublesome bathroom and shower doors have been replaced by curtains, the sink is accessible, the toilet is flanked by adjustable grab bars, and one can roll into the shower since there is no threshold (Figure 10.4). Accessibility at the National Rehabilitation Hospital—whether it means going unassisted to the bathroom or being lowered into the therapeutic pool in a

FIGURE 10.1
Front of the National Rehabilitation Hospital. Garage entrance is to the left.

FIGURE 10.2
National Rehabilitation Hospital reception
desk with lowered counter. The atrium is
beyond the desk.

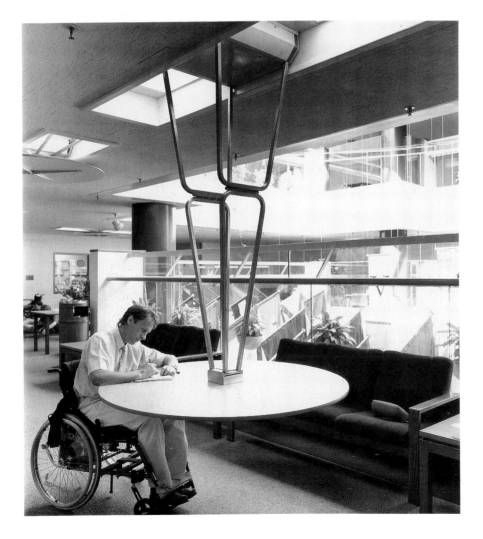

FIGURE 10.3
National Rehabilitation Hospital second
floor atrium. Suspended table in foreground.
Price Baum, who is sitting at the table, does
not use a pen, but the photographer
inappropriately suggested it as a prop. Note
the raised table at the upper left.

FIGURE 10.4
National Rehabilitation Hospital patient bathroom with roll-in shower to left. The right grab bar is not visible. The absence of a threshold and the use of curtains rather than doors make this bathroom more accessible than those in other facilities.

seat rather than a sling*—preserves and enhances the self-image of someone recovering from a disabling illness or accident (Figure 10.5).

Architect Mariani brought coherence to the individual elements of accessibility by making natural lighting the unifying and uplifting theme of the hospital. On entering the lobby, one's eye is drawn to the central, skylit atrium. The public spaces on all four floors are organized around and bathed in the light of the atrium. Major spaces not adjacent to the atrium have their own sources of natural lighting; the therapeutic recreation room has a glass ceiling (Figure 10.6). The architectural aesthetic reinforces the medical program. The National Rehabilitation Hospital's building and grounds will be complete once the therapeutic recreation garden planned for the east end of the site is built.

*Lacking the rigidity of the chair, the sling moves back and forth, appearing unsafe and undignified. Some people refuse to use a sling to get into a pool.

FIGURE 10.5
National Rehabilitation Hospital pool, seat lift, and stairs into pool.

FIGURE 10.6
National Rehabilitation Hospital therapautic recreation room, with natural lighting.

At the Washington Home and Hospice, two gardens are not merely complements to the complex, they are the major elements. The Barbara Bush Garden, which honors her 20 years of volunteering at the home, is a small formal garden in the central courtyard. The garden's focus is a water fountain, bracketed by plant and flower beds. The flower and plant bed walls are low, enabling patients in wheelchairs to touch and smell the plantings as well as see them. Sitting on the low walls or benches, nondisabled visitors are next to and at the same height as a patient in a wheelchair. The Bush Garden is surrounded by the home's dining room and major corridors, and can be seen from upper story rooms, so it may be enjoyed even by residents who do not go into it (Figure 10.7). The Hospice Garden, which effectively screens the patients and building from the Home's parking lot, is much less formal, less defined than the Barbara Bush Garden. Hospice patients are wheeled in their beds or wheelchairs into the adjacent garden where they have the soothing sounds of the water fountain and the sight, touch, and smell of the flowers (Figures 10.8 and 10.9). Steven Mackler, of the

FIGURE 10.7
Barbara Bush Garden at Washington Home and Hospice.

FIGURE 10.8
Hospice Garden at Washington Home and Hospice.

Landscape Group, Inc., succeeded admirably in designing two gardens adapted to people in wheelchairs.

Pascal Pittman, AIA of Oudens + Knoop Architects PC, designed the 3-year-old new facility of the Washington Home and Hospice to "maintain the patient's sense of dignity" by providing safe, varied public spaces and private rooms decorated with personal furnishings. He created transitional areas at the intersection of corridors so that a patient could stay in a semienclosed, nonthreatening space until he or she was ready to move into a larger, more open public space. Within the individual patient room the central area is left for wheelchair access and the patient's own furniture and the hospital bed are along the walls (Figure 10.10). The windows in the rooms and at the ends of corridors have been placed to give the most pleasing vistas.

Dr. Jared Falek, executive director of the Washington Home and Hospice said "our gardens, which surround the home and are inside, are a natural part of our program, something which many of our clients use almost every day." Falek and his designers succeeded in creating a garden within the city, on a site crowded by over-

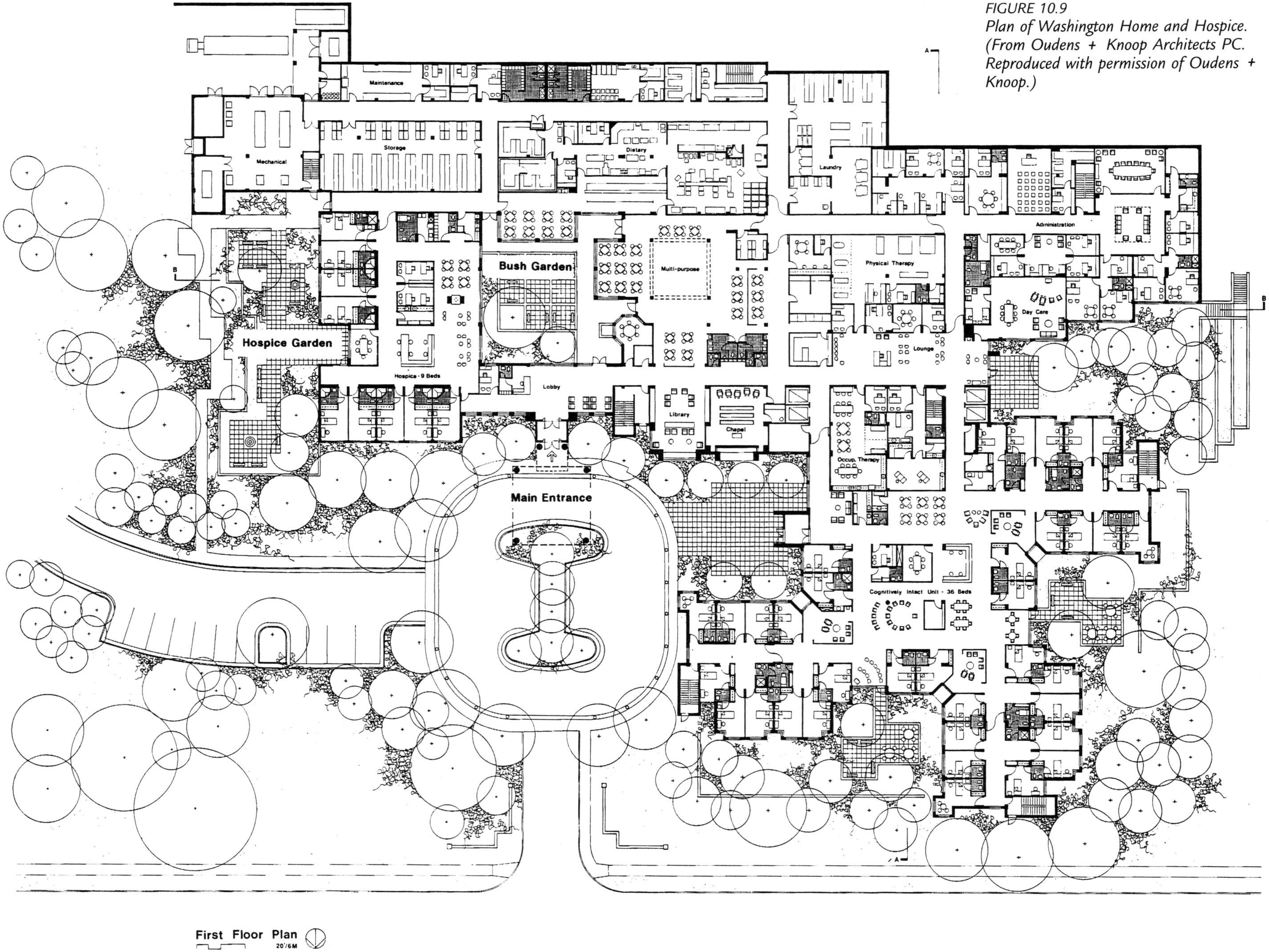

FIGURE 10.9
Plan of Washington Home and Hospice.
(From Oudens + Knoop Architects PC.
Reproduced with permission of Oudens +
Knoop.)

First Floor Plan

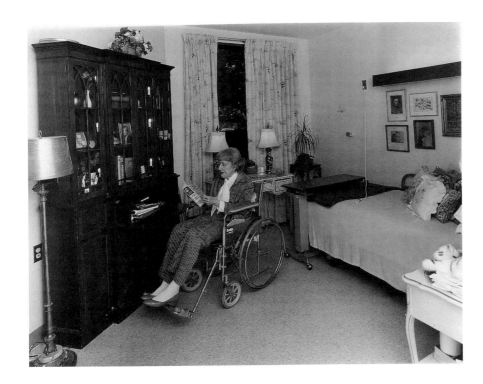

FIGURE 10.10
Washington Home patient's room,
decorated with mementos and furniture she
brought from her house.

whelming institutional buildings and parking lots, to the great benefit of the Home and Hospice's residents.

One intuitively expects a medical facility to be accessible and to be a healthful environment. The reality is that some hospitals place rehabilitation departments in basements and put patients in rooms with inaccessible bathrooms. Mayer Spivack, of Harvard Medical School, wrote that "hospitals and prisons are the only environments in the U.S. culture (as far as we know) that are in danger of being so mismanaged that they can drive people crazy." (Mayer Spivack in *Institutional Settings: An Environmental Design Approach*, edited by Joanna Tamer. Human Sciences Press, New York, 1984, p. 21.) When, however, medical facilities are designed and managed with the patient's physical and psychological well-being as paramount considerations, and accessibility is an integral element in the program, the results are places like the National Rehabilitation Hospital and the Washington Home and Hospice.

Section V

MUSEUMS

Providing accessibility at museums housed in historic buildings is probably the most difficult challenge created by the Americans with Disabilities Act.* The drafters of the ADA regulations anticipated this problem and specifically addressed historic preservation issues in the regulations (No. 36.405, Appendix A.4.1.7). The officials responsible for enforcing the ADA regulations have subsequently spoken at forums such as the 1992 meeting of the American Association of Museums (AAM) to reassure museum administrators concerning the affects of the ADA on them. The audience at the AAM meeting seemed unconvinced, but it can take comfort and learn from the accessibility accommodations some museums have already made.

The Smithsonian Institution has taken its most architecturally impressive building, the Castle, and made it physically accessible without diminishing its exterior architectural statement. On the inside, the Castle is now a visitor information center filled with accessible displays to help visitors know what each Smithsonian museum offers. Even the display cases are compatible with the interior's intact mid-nineteenth-century details. Without compromising either the interior or the exterior, the Smithsonian made the building physically accessible, and its exhibits provide information that is accessible to all visitors, regardless of disabilities.

Even the relatively small Historical Society of Washington made its late nineteenth-century house museum physically accessible without compromising it.

Sometimes a building has too much significance to be altered to create physical accessibility. At the Statue of Liberty and Independence National Historical Park, the National Park Service created accessible programs as an alternative to making the structures accessible. (That the National Park Service was willing to alter Ellis Island,

---

*Museums receiving federal funds were already required to be accessible under the Rehabilitation Act of 1973, a requirement largely ignored.

which was restored at the same time as the Statue of Liberty, to make it completely accessible suggests that the rationale for deciding which structures are so important that they cannot be made physically accessible is in flux.)

Boston's Museum of Science is hardly historic, but it cannot afford to redo every inaccessible exhibit. Instead it creates new accessible exhibits to augment the original inaccessible ones. The museum is most notable for its continuing efforts to improve its accessibility—always learning from experiments. Accessibility is seen as a dynamic process rather than a static goal.

Even for museums committed to accessibility, key issues remain unresolved. Experts on vision impairment disagree on whether braille should be used and if black type on a white background is better than white type on a dark background. Curators want low light levels to protect the objects while higher light levels are needed for people with visual disabilities. (Some recent Washington exhibitions have had light levels too low even for people without any visual disabilities.)

No museum adequately informs visitors of available accessibility features. Visitors with disabilities are expected to inquire at an information desk. But often the representatives behind the desk do not know, give out erroneous information, or cannot find the brochure describing the accessible features. Also it is improper to put the burden on the visitor with the disability to find out what is available. Museums need to have signs, audible announcements, and prominent displays of brochures and charts describing accessible features.

Even if a museum and its exhibits can be made accessible, is accessibility detrimental to the exhibits and the nondisabled visitor? The National Building Museum and the Museum of Science convincingly demonstrate that the opposite is true. Many of the features that make exhibitions better for people with disabilities make them more comprehensible and enjoyable for people without disabilities.

Administrators of small museums might think that accessibility solutions used by the large, wealthy, national institutions such as the National Park Service and the Smithsonian are not applicable. But the National Park Service and Smithsonian also deal with much more important architectural and engineering landmarks and if they can appropriately make them accessible, then the small museums should be encouraged. Less expensive, less extensive versions of the physical and communication accessibility methods discussed in this section are applicable to smaller museums.

Achieving museum accessibility is more complex than the ADA regulations suggest, something that museum administrators have already figured out. Museum accessibility is a subtle, nearly infinitely variable, not yet fully explored, mixture of physical and program accessibility. If done correctly it can increase everyone's enjoyment of museums.

Chapter 11

MUSEUM OF SCIENCE

Serious architectural guidebooks to Boston ignore the always crowded Museum of Science. Its nonaesthetic subject matter, undistinguished location, and hodgepodge of post–World War II architecture apparently do not meet the standards of architectural writers. These critics are missing the obvious: the museum's architecture is an (unintended) metaphor for its dynamic, inclusive philosophy which makes the museum immensely popular and a model of program accessibility.

Walter Muir Whitehill, late director of the Boston Athenaeum and one of the city's most literate twentieth-century intellectuals, skipped the Museum of Science in his *Topographical History of Boston*. He did, however, describe the elegant, Second Empire style headquarters, built in 1864, of the museum's precursor, the Boston Society of Natural History. Once the society decided to display more branches of science than natural history, changed its name, and moved out of Boston's Back Bay to a larger site, Whitehill and subsequent architectural writers seem to have lost interest.

That topography and aesthetics are very important to Bostonians is a disadvantage to the Museum of Science. They think of their city in terms of sections: Beacon Hill, the Back Bay, the South End, etc. The Museum of Science is, however, in an amorphous, undefined area—half in Boston, half in Cambridge. The site lacks the requisite visual identity and cachet of the city's other neighborhoods. On this less than ideal (although free) location, starting in 1948, the museum was built in sections, with the most recent one—completed in 1987—designed by Stubbins Associates. As a result of its sporadic growth, the museum consists of interlocked buildings, each reflecting the architectural tastes of the decade in which it was built. Finally, Bostonians—and perhaps most Americans—view art museums, not their science museums, as important to their cultural heritage. It is remarkable that the Museum of Science is so popular, considering that it was built in the wrong part of Boston, lacks heroic architecture, and displays the wrong artifacts.

People probably take their children to the museum to encourage an interest in science, but they (children and parents) enjoy it and return for the very reasons the aesthetes disdain it. At the museum, there is a hands-on, interactive, flashing-light excitement that no art museum offers. From the microscopic to the electric, to the electronic, to the natural historic, to the astronomic, the exhibits involve, challenge, and energize visitors regardless of age. For those temporarily exhausted by the displays, the glass wall of the museum's central bay offers an unparalleled view of sailboats on the Charles River, and the Back Bay's nineteenth-century church spires and residences along the river. For those exhausted and hungry, there is the retreat to the museum's restaurant with nearly as dramatic a view of the Charles.

Long ago, the museum realized it had to entertain in order to "expose/kindle/stimulate" the visitor. In a May 1970 fund raising letter, the museum director wrote that exhibits were to be fun and were to "involve the visitor either intellectually or physically . . . give him control of the operation of an exhibit (a hand crank instead of push button) . . . let him experience the process of inquiry and discovery." The male and nondisabled orientation of the 1970 letter are absent in the 1991 mission statement which more fully and more broadly defines the museum's purpose and intended audience: "The mission of the Museum of Science is to stimulate interest in and further understanding of science and technology and their importance for individuals and society . . . " and the museum is "dedicated to attracting the broadest possible spectrum of participants, and involving them in activities, exhibits and programs which will . . . respect individual interests, backgrounds and abilities. . . ." During the last twenty years, the museum's programs have become more inclusive, while still working within the restraints of buildings and permanent exhibitions built for a less inclusive approach.

The first section of the museum that most visitors experience is the five-story parking garage, which is inaccessible, as it lacks an elevator. But in front of the garage entrance, signs warn of its inaccessibility and direct cars with a driver or passenger with a disability to park on the museum's driveway. The person with a disability still needs to cross the driveway to the museum's entrance. This new accessible entrance wing, which opened in 1987, has automatically opening doors.

The museum resolves building inaccessibility by either building a new, accessible feature (e.g., the new main entrance wing) or by providing an accessible alternative to an inaccessible feature (e.g., allowing disabled visitors to park on the driveway rather than in the inaccessible parking garage). The same two-alternative approach to making the building accessible is used in making exhibitions accessible. The dioramas of the New England Habitats exhibition, for example, are only accessible to visitors who can see the posed ani-

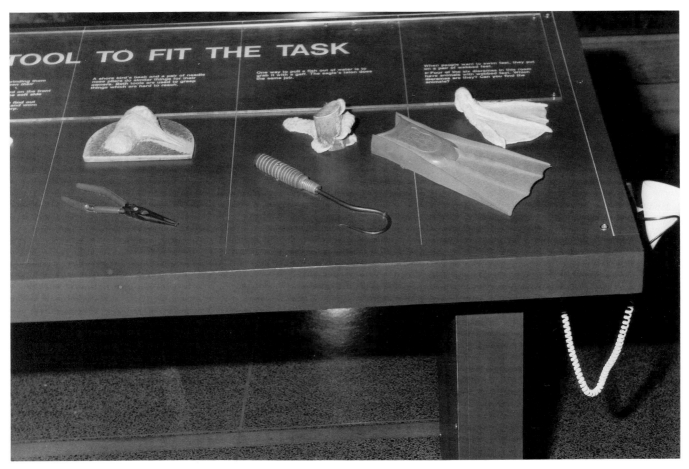

TOOL TO FIT THE TASK

FIGURE 11.1
Partial view of display table "A Tool to Fit the Task," which uses tactile models, highly legible signage, and an audio message to show the similarity between animal features and tools. This display table is in front of a diorama of the New England Habitats exhibit.

mals behind glass. And even for the sighted, it is a static exhibit, which only briefly holds a visitor's interest. By placing new un-enclosed display tables a few feet in front of the glass cases, with highly legible signage and additional animals, the exhibition be-came more sensory, more interesting, and more informative—without changing the dioramas. The display tables allow visitors to examine animal skins under a microscope, to touch and compare animal features to a fabricated tool, such as a bird's beak to a pair of pliers. Each display table also has an audible explanation (Figure 11.1). But visitors are not limited to examining animal features. Three complete specimens—a small bear, a beaver, and a cormorant—are also on display to be touched (Figure 11.2). The sign at the exhibit nicely sums up the museum's approach to exhibit acces-sibility: "People enjoy using their senses. Some people rely mostly on sight, while others rely on hearing or sense of touch. We want New England Habitats to be more enjoyable for all visitors, includ-ing those with disabilities. That's why you will find things to touch, hear, see and smell in this exhibit."

Although the new displays at the New England Habitats were tested by students from the Perkins School for the Blind (see Chap-ter 9), an accessibility mistake was made. Although the angle of the eyepiece of the microscope for examining animal skins is adjustable

Please touch this beaver very gent
so that others can enjoy this exhib

FIGURE 11.2
*A road kill is now a tactile display at the
New England Habitats.*

to suit people standing or in wheelchairs, the position of the table leg makes access to the microscope difficult for someone in a wheelchair. Learning from that early effort at accessibility, the museum now mounts exhibits on tables so that the legs don't block access and the table height can be adjusted to the height of the person in the wheelchair (Figure 11.3). All new exhibits such as the microscope table in Figure 11.3 are given a trial run in the "test tube" room, where museum staff observe and question children using the exhibits. Based on these insights, new exhibitions can be further refined before being permanently placed in an exhibition hall. Making exhibitions more accessible and more informative is an unending process at the museum.

To help people with limited vision find exhibitions with tactile features and better enjoy the entire museum, a recorded tour, braille handouts, and an enlarged-print floor plan are available from the information desk at the entrance. The museum's planetarium also has a braille brochure and tactile astronomy illustrations; the museum's Omni Theater has enhanced descriptive narration for some movies. The theater also has amplified headsets for people who are hearing impaired. An interesting dichotomy exists in the museum's accessibility techniques for the people with limited vision: the museum's braille brochure directs the visually impaired to the New England Habitats exhibit, but no braille signage is used in the exhibit (because relatively few people who are visually impaired read braille).

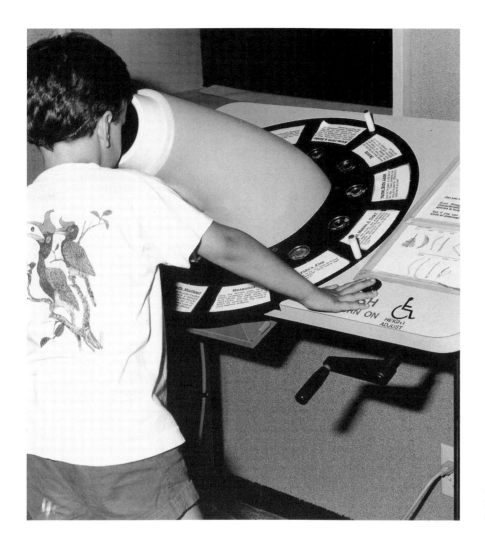

FIGURE 11.3
New exhibition with height adjustable for wheelchairs being tested by a visitor in the museum's temporary exhibit space.

Only a museum unconcerned with criticism would tolerate the stylistically disparate facades that the Museum of Science has erected. But one expects a science museum to take risks—in the scientific theories it demonstrates, in its exhibits, and even in its approaches to accessibility. However, the museum always aspires to be intellectually accessible. It has come to understand—and can teach other museums—that physical accessibility is a precursor to intellectual accessibility.

Chapter 12

THE SMITHSONIAN INSTITUTION

The Smithsonian hosts some 27 million visitors annually. Many of them arrive knowing little more than that the Smithsonian is on the Mall. The tourists have seen photographs of the castle, heard of the Air and Space Museum and the Hope Diamond, but few know how many museums constitute the Smithsonian, exactly where they are, and what they display. To help these lost souls, the Smithsonian Institution converted the main floor of the castle—the Smithsonian's landmark and one of Washington, D.C.'s best known symbols—into a visitors' center.

The castle, built from 1846 to 1855 of Seneca sandstone, occupies the most visible site on the mall, midway between the United States Capitol, the east terminus of the mall, and the Washington Monument, the west terminus. The castle's picturesque, irregular profile stands out against the Washington skyline, and from anywhere on the mall and especially from the west front of the Capitol, a visitor's eye is drawn to the castle. Its prominent architecture and location made the castle the logical choice to be the Smithsonian's Visitor Information and Associates' Reception Center.

Prior to its closing in late 1987 for renovations, the castle housed exhibits on Washington, D.C. on its main floor and administrative offices, including the prestigious Woodrow Wilson Center, on the upper floors. The castle reopened in November 1989 as the visitors' center. The Smithsonian intended the renovated castle to be an architectural symbol of its commitment to its visitors:

> The decision to establish the Smithsonian Information Center demonstrates the Institution's recognition of the public's need for information and orientation assistance and reaffirms its commitment to making Smithsonian facilities and activities readily accessible. The Information Center will provide visitors with the opportunity to gain the knowledge needed to make informed choices about the use of their time at the Smithsonian and will save them the frustration of an aimless trek from building to building.

FIGURE 12.1
*North elevation of the Smithsonian
Institution's castle, as seen from the Mall.*

Approximately 1.3 people a year visit the Information Center and
the total is expected to reach 3 million per year.

At the time the castle was being rehabilitated, the Smithsonian
established a central office on accessibility. Its director, Jan Majewski, worked closely with Mary Grace Potter, director of the Information Center, and her designers to assure that the castle would be
fully accessible: physically and informationally.

Physical accessibility was achieved mostly through modest
changes. The main entrances to the castle are in its north tower,
which has doors on the front and on the east and west sides (Figure
12.1). The front doors were not changed; the east and west entrances were altered to provide accessibility. At the west entrance on
the north tower, automatic doors and a ramp, with railings compatible with the building's architecture, were added (Figure 12.2).
The east entrance's landscaped, ascending walk to the entrance
steps echoes the west entrance ramp. Inside the north tower, a text
telephone and accessible drinking fountain have been installed.
Also, the openings from the north tower to the building's main
exhibition space have been increased from one to three.

At the west end of the main room, accessible bathrooms were
created. The men's room has a wide stall with grab bars, a lowered
urinal, and counters with knee space. Wheelchair circulation
would, however, be better if the large trash can was removed. Also,
if both sinks had lever handles and padded waste pipe, there would

FIGURE 12.2
Accessible ramp and automatic doors on west side of north tower. Wooden enclosure is temporary.

FIGURE 12.3
Castle's men's room with clear knee space under both sinks, but only right sink has lever handles and padded pipes. The trash can at right is a needless obstacle to wheelchair circulation.

not be the appearance of separate but equal facilities (Figure 12.3). A ramp was also installed to the staff and associate dining room west of the accessible bathrooms. At the east end of the main room, two small, wheelchair-accessible theaters were built. Next to the benches at the front of the each theater there is space for people using wheelchairs, and if more room is needed the benches can be removed. The rear of the theater has fixed, row seating. Each theater shows short introductory movies on the Smithsonian museums. One theater has closed audio loop and its movie is captioned, but there is no sign to inform the hearing impaired of these features. (If audio loops had been installed in both theaters their signals would have interfered with each other.) Beyond the main exhibition hall is the south tower, housing the restored children's museum room of 1902. A temporary ramp links the south tower to the garden behind the castle. The Enid A. Haupt Garden, designed by Sasaki Associates, has recently been resurfaced to improve accessibility for people in wheelchairs or pushing strollers (Figure 12.4). (For comparison, see Chapter 20 on Charleston's Waterfront Park.) Eventually, an opening to the elevator in the south tower will be cut in the northwest wall of the children's museum room. The elevator will provide wheelchair access from the children's room up to the main exhibition hall.

Within the main exhibition hall, wheelchair-accessible displays provide informational accessibility for visitors. Enclosed in display cases, suitably elaborate and massive to match the castle's architecture, touch screen monitors (in several languages) and an electronic wall map help visitors locate the various museums and learn about

FIGURE 12.4
Entrance to south tower of castle, with temporary ramp.

their collections (Figures 12.5 and 12.6). The monitors are mounted at different heights to assure easy use by people in wheelchairs or who are short, as well as by visitors of average height. The electronic wall map has ample knee space for people in wheelchairs as do the two scale models of Washington, D.C. One model is tactile, employing three-dimensional building forms and contrasting colors and textures, along with braille, to aid the visitor who is visually impaired (Figure 12.7). Two computer monitors using an extra large typeface display the daily events at the museums. For any visitor still confused, there are also backlighted displays, volunteers at an information desk who answer questions and provide brochures (including "A Guide for Disabled Visitors"), and of course the guards at the entrances.

The castle offers visitors a variety of entertaining ways to learn about the Smithsonian; ranging from the entirely passive (watching a movie) to the interactive (touch screen monitors). They are accessible to anyone in a wheelchair and require little manual dexterity.

FIGURE 12.5
Touch screen monitors at two heights for wheelchair accessibility.

FIGURE 12.6
Electronic wall map with clear knee space and monitors at two heights.

FIGURE 12.7
Scaled tactile map of the mall, using contrasting textures and colors, braille. The table has clear knee space.

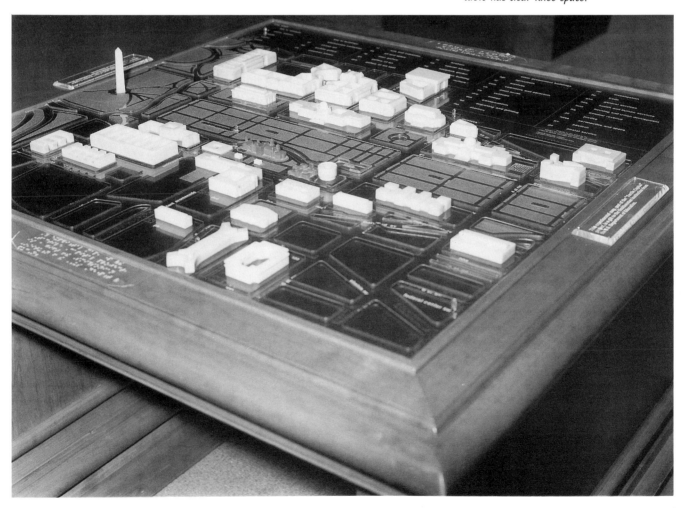

FIGURE 12.8
Wheelchair-height automated teller machine at the entrance to the education building at the National Zoo.

The accessible features at the various Smithsonian facilities reflect federal accessibility standards and the architectural character of each institution. Other Smithsonian museums on the mall and the National Zoo, for example, have automated teller machines accessible to someone in a wheelchair (Figure 12.8). But such a machine would be incompatible with the castle's nineteenth-century ambiance and would irreparably damage the historic fabric. Automatic toilets, urinals, and faucets with concealed pipes, are appropriate for the National Zoo, but not for the castle (Figure 12.9). By enclosing late-twentieth-century high-tech electronic displays in mid-nineteenth-century-style furniture, the Smithsonian left intact the popular image of the castle as a pristine nineteenth-century architectural landmark.

Scholars and critics share the public's high regard for the castle. Architect and tour guide writer Richard Saul Wurman described the castle as "widely recognized as one of the finest Gothic Revival buildings in America. . . ." Designed by James Renwick (1818–1895), who is best remembered for St. Patrick's Cathedral in New York City, the castle was designated a National Historic Landmark nearly 30 years ago. The castle is of sufficient architectural importance to have its own office of architectural history.

The Smithsonian architectural historians, along with those of four other city and federal historic preservation offices, had to approve the accessibility modifications to the castle. (Theoretically, most of the agencies only had a review role, but in fact, their ap-

FIGURE 12.9
Automatic faucet and concealed pipes in a men's room at the National Zoo.

proval was needed.) The extent of preservationist involvement in the castle renovation is unique, but under the ADA, accessibility modifications to a designated landmark must respect the building's historic character.

With the exception of the temporary rear ramp, no accessibility feature that was added to either the exterior or the interior of the castle distracts from the architectural power of the building. In fact, the new display cases for the accessible exhibits better relate to the castle's interior volume and detailing than the previous exhibit cases. Furthermore, the new ramp and sloped walkway flanking the north tower make access to the building easier and, to the degree they are noted, they emphasize the centrality and prominence of the north tower. At its oldest and most distinguished building, the Smithsonian Institution demonstrated that it is on the cutting edge of accessibility in information systems and buildings.

Chapter 13

NATIONAL BUILDING MUSEUM

Judiciary Square is home to two of the U.S. Capitol's most unusual memorials. The National Law Enforcement Officers Memorial, dedicated in October 1991, was built around two subway elevators and an escalator. Across the street is the Pension Building, the most interesting and bizarre of architectural memorials erected after the Civil War to honor the Union troops. Erected in the 1880s ostensibly to house civil servants paying pensions to Civil War veterans or their survivors, the Pension Building now houses the National Building Museum on its first and second floors. That museum's permanent exhibition on Washington, D.C. was specifically designed for the visually impaired and blind. The efforts to make accessible the National Building Museum, the Pension Building, the National Law Enforcement Officers Memorial, and the subway demonstrate the apparent simplicity, yet underlying difficulty of providing integrated accessibility (Figure 13.1).

The National Building Museum mounts its temporary exhibits on the first floor of the Pension Building and its two permanent exhibitions on the second floor (Figure 13.2). One permanent exhibit details the history of the construction of the building and profiles its designer, U.S. Army Engineer, General Montgomery C. Meigs. The second permanent exhibit, *Washington: Symbol and City*, done in collaboration with the American Foundation for the Blind, explores through several media the Capitol's public monuments and anonymous neighborhoods. Although created for and in consultation with the visually impaired and blind community, the exhibition is also intended to be attractive to museum visitors who are not visually impaired.

In subtle, but important ways *Washington: Symbol and City* is different from exhibitions in other museums. Most museum exhibits are free-form, allowing the visitor to choose a direction to go in each gallery—left or right—even in exhibits intended to be seen in a certain order. But at *Washington: Symbol and City*, the viewer feels

FIGURE 13.1
National Law Enforcement Officers
Memorial, with subway elevators in center.
Animal sculptures mark beginning of one of
two low walls with names of killed officers.
The Pension Building is in the background.

FIGURE 13.2
Interior of the Pension Building looking
east.

compelled to move along the galleries' walls in a prescribed path. At other museums, the walls are merely the backdrops on which paintings are hung and are the distant backgrounds for free-standing sculpture and display cases. But at *Washington: Symbol and City,* the explanations, graphics, enormous photographic murals, and three-dimensional objects emanate from the wall. Even the free-standing, large scale models of the monuments and rowhouses are connected to the walls by three raised strips on the carpet (Figure 13.3). A visually impaired or blind person would look at and/or feel the wall and objects and then be guided by the tracks to the model. Since the visually impaired or blind museum visitors would approach the model from the wall, the front of the building (with a braille label) faces the wall, while the back of the building (with a nonraised label) faces away from the wall (Figures 13.3 and 13.4). The models have been simplified to prevent what Ed Ruch, consultant to the exhibition from the American Foundation for the Blind, describes as information overload for the visually impaired and blind. A guide rail on the wall intended for the visually impaired and blind reinforces for the sighted visitor the message that one views the exhibit by moving along the wall (Figure 13.5); the guide rail is intended to provide the defining edge needed by the visually im-

FIGURE 13.3
Scale model of the White House, showing south (rear) facade with printed label on guide rail. On the floor at left, three tracks lead to the wall. Photographic mural and objects from the White House are in the background.

FIGURE 13.4
Scale model of the White House, showing north (front) facade with braille label facing the wall.

Aquia sandstone with mason's mark

FIGURE 13.5
White House stone, with braille and printed labels on guide rail.

paired and blind (see Chapter 9), but, according to a museum guide, people tap their canes against the base of the wall, ignoring the guide rail.

At the recommendation of consultants on visual impairment, *Washington: Symbol and City* relies on a 90-minute audiotape, which repeats all the wall text and describes everything in the exhibit, to help convey the exhibition to the visually impaired and blind. To allow the visitor to go at his or her own pace, the tape machine is controlled by the user. In some other museums, by contrast, the tape plays automatically, and the user has no control. A 90-minute audiotape is probably too detailed for the nondisabled visitor, as most museum visitors do not have the patience or interest to read long texts or to decipher complex displays. For most visitors who are visually impaired or blind, the comprehensive descriptions on the tape are appreciated, regardless of their length. (The National Building Museum is considering preparing a shorter version of the tape.) The audiotape is augmented by simple braille identifications and limited large print wall text. No raised lettering is used, although the tactile map has raised numerals. The vision-impairment consultants were evenly divided as to whether dark type on a light background or light type on a dark background is better for the wall text, so the exhibit uses both arrangements. Wall surfaces have dull finishes to reduce glare, and the overhead lighting is even to avoid creating shadows.

Large photographic wall murals provide a dramatic backdrop for the models and give visual unity to each section of the exhibition for the nonimpaired visitor and for the person with limited vision. The murals also enable people with limited vision to see details that would otherwise not be legible.

Only the two large early-twentieth-century models of Washington, which are behind glass, cannot be directly sensed by someone who is blind or has little vision, but they are accessible through the description on the tape.

Washington: Symbol and City demonstrates that an exhibition designed to meet the needs of the visually impaired and blind (information available by touch, sight, and hearing; unambiguous layouts; well-lit spaces; succinct text; and a carefully limited number of objects on display) is equally suited for visitors without visual disabilities. Making the exhibition accessible to the visually disabled and blind did not make it any less accessible or interesting for the nondisabled.

The National Building Museum's permanent exhibitions could, however, have been installed to be more easily accessible to someone like Eddie (see Chapter 1), who is blind and in a wheelchair. Placing objects such as the U.S. Capitol baluster and modillion (Figure 13.6) at the junction of two walls, forces someone in a wheelchair to do extra maneuvering to get out of the corner after touching the objects. Also, the upper portions of the angled tactile map might be beyond the touch of someone in a wheelchair (Figure 13.7). More troublesome is the placement of the most important

FIGURE 13.6
U.S. Capitol artifacts displayed too close to
a corner, making wheelchair access
needlessly difficult.

Baluster, U.S. Capitol
Modillion, U.S. Capitol

FIGURE 13.7
Wall mounted, angled tactile map with
raised structures, roads, and numerals. High
contrast lettering and braille labels make
the map accessible to visitors who are blind
or have limited vision.

Mall, 1991
1. U.S. Capitol
2. Union Station
3. U.S. Supreme Court
4. Library of Congress
5. Museum
6. Pennsylvania Avenue
7. Federal Triangle
8. White House
9. Washington Monument
10. Jefferson Memorial
11. Vietnam Veterans Memorial
12. Lincoln Memorial

exhibitions—the permanent exhibitions—on the second floor, which requires people with mobility disabilities to depend on elevators and requires all people to travel farther than they would if the exhibitions were on the first floor. By reserving the first floor for temporary exhibits, the National Building Museum can incorporate the courtyard into such exhibitions and it does not have to raise and lower heavy, temporary exhibition pieces to and from the second floor. But as *Washington: Symbol and City* is specifically designed for people with visual disabilities, it should have been placed on the first floor to be more accessible to people with multiple disabilities.

Access to the National Building Museum's permanent exhibitions is not ideal, but it is far better than the access to the Pension Building which houses the National Building Museum. The Pension Building has an entrance in the middle of each of its facades. The entrance on the east side faces the building's parking lot, with loading platform, and designated disabled parking spaces. On the north side, it is two steps up from the sidewalk to a long concrete path across a lawn and then one step up from the path to the building's outer doors. In the vestibule between the outer and inner doors, there is a permanent ramp, without handrails. On the building's west side, a temporary exterior ramp leads to the outer doors and a second temporary ramp leads to the inner doors. But a guard has to be summoned by a bell to unlock the doors. The outside ramp to the west entrance connects to a path to the south sidewalk, which has a wide curbcut (originally a driveway cut) a few feet from the path. On the south side of the building, the sidewalk and short path to the building are on the same level. It is then three steps from the path to the outer doors and then three more steps in the vestibule to the inner doors. The south entrance is closest to the sidewalk, closest to the subway elevators and (along with the north entrance) closest to the Pension Building's elevators. The south portal (with added ramps, handrails, automatic door, and curbcut), therefore, is the most logical entrance for *both* the nondisabled and disabled (Figure 13.8).

Yet the north rather than the south is designated to become the permanent accessible entrance. The north entrance can be made the most formal of the four entrances as the lawn is sufficiently wide to cut a driveway for limousines bringing important people to presidential inaugural balls held at the Pension Building. The President, important guests, and people with mobility disabilities would drive directly to the canopied door and then enter through the accessible entrance. As a permanent ramp is already in place, only handrails are needed. (Automatic door controls would be quite helpful.) To add ramps to the south entrance, by contrast, would alter or conceal the historic fabric of the stairs. (This is the same problem that the Smithsonian is wresting with on the south entrance to the Castle, see Chapter 12.) The National Building Museum, as client, and the General Services Administration, as building manager, chose the formal, pro-preservation solution rather than the more equitable, convenient solution for disabled visitors traveling by subway.

A ramped entrance is but one of the accessibility measures taken by the General Services Administration to comply with the Uniform Federal Accessibility Standards for federal buildings, prepared by the General Services Administration, Department of Defense, U.S. Postal Service, and Department of Housing and Urban Development. The Pension Building's drinking fountains and bathrooms have been made wheelchair accessible and two fire-safe emergency staging areas have been created where people unable to descend the stairs would wait to be rescued (Figure 13.9).

Each facility at Judiciary Square accommodates the disabled, but each has a different emphasis. The subway station has elevators for people with mobility disabilities, but the entire subway system has been criticized for not adequately meeting the needs of the visually impaired and blind. Specifically, vision-impairment experts

FIGURE 13.8
South, public entrance to the Pension Building and National Building Museum.

FIGURE 13.9
Looking from second floor corridor to emergency staging area with fire-resistant doors closed. Area has emergency voice communicator.

argue that the warning strip at the edge of the subway platform is neither sufficiently wide nor texturally distinctive enough to warn a visually impaired or blind person that he or she is approaching the platform edge.

The National Law Enforcement Officers Memorial, designed by Davis Buckley, AIA, is also accessible for someone in a wheelchair, but does not address the needs of the visually impaired.

Once inside the Pension Building, the General Service Administration provides accessible accommodations, but getting into the building is neither as convenient nor dignified as it could be. The National Building Museum's *Washington: Symbol and City* precisely serves both the blind and visually impaired visitor and the visitor who is not visually impaired, yet the placement of some objects and the second story location of the permanent exhibitions are less considerate of visitors with mobility disabilities. (Many people have more than one disability.) The accessible ensemble of subway, police officers memorial, Pension Building, and National Building Museum's *Washington: Symbol and City* is rare, perhaps unique; a person with a mobility, visual, or communications disability can get to the memorials by public transportation, and in the case of National Building Museum's exhibit experience it as fully as the nondisabled visitor. However, the most accessible route between components was overlooked.

Chapter 14

NATIONAL PARK SERVICE

With the Statue of Liberty, Ellis Island, and Independence National Historical Park, the National Park Service is responsible for perhaps the best known symbols of American liberty. These cultural sites are also architectural or engineering masterpieces. In restoring them, the National Park Service balanced accessibility requirements and historic preservation requirements.

Since at least the bicentennial celebration of the Declaration of Independence in 1976, the National Park Service, an agency of the U.S. Department of the Interior, has formally worked to make national monuments more accessible. On May 11, 1976, a ceremony was held at the Lincoln Memorial to dedicate the newly installed elevator for disabled visitors. In his proclamation read by a spokesman at the ceremony, President Gerald Ford repeatedly emphasized the diversity of the American population, and went on to state,

> As we lay the cornerstone of America's Third Century, I am most happy to commend the Department of the Interior and the Architectural and Transportation Barrier Compliance Board on the inauguration of the special Bicentennial program to help make our national monuments more accessible to our handicapped fellow citizens. Efforts such as this are helping to make our great national celebration a memorable and meaningful one for all.

The National Park Service also cut approximately 200 curbcuts along the mall and adjacent park, installed an elevator and ramps at the Jefferson Memorial, and designated handicap parking at Washington, Lincoln, and Jefferson Memorials, along the National Mall, and at the Smithsonian's National Air and Space Museum.

Three years later, in 1979, the National Park Service increased its efforts to make all its sites accessible (now consisting of more than 350 memorials, monuments, battlefields, seashores, natural areas, etc.) by creating a Division of Special Programs and Populations. The Park Service's accessibility policy was formally articulated in a 1983 directive:

> In planning, construction, and renovation of buildings and facilities and in the provision of programs and services to the public and employees, it is policy of the National Park Service to provide the highest level of accessibility possible and feasible for persons with visual, hearing, mobility, and mental impairments, consistent with the obligation to conserve park resources and preserve the quality of the park experience for everyone.

The following principles are key to this policy:

- The Park Service is committed to accessibility for its employees as well as the public at natural as well as made sites.
- The Park Service will not create separate facilities for the disabled, but will make accessibility changes that enable a person with a disability to have the same experience as a nondisabled person.
- The Park Service will not diminish the resource to provide accessibility.

A January 1990 policy statement explicitly addresses accessibility modifications to its historic buildings:

> The National Park Service will provide the highest feasible level of physical access for disabled persons to historic properties consistent with the preservation of the properties' significant historical attributes. Access modifications for disabled persons will be designed and installed to least affect the features of a property that contribute to its significance. Some impairment of some features will be accepted in providing access. If it is determined that modification of particular features would destroy a property's significance, however, such modifications will not be made.

The Park Service has been involved longer in accessibility issues and its accessibility policies more fully articulated than those of many other organizations. Does that mean that Park Service's most important museums and historic properties are more accessible, yet better preserved? The answer is an unqualified yes.

Independence National Historical Park, Philadelphia, has two visitor brochures of nearly identical size. One is the usual National Park Service brochure with dense text, in small type, explaining the site's history, complemented by colorful drawings, photographs, and map. The other brochure, labeled "Accessibility at Independence National Historical Park" has much larger type, much less verbiage, no small photographs or drawings, and only uses black, white, and green. The buildings on the map are depicted at a size nearly twice as large as on the other brochure. In addition to being a simplified, high-contrast brochure, much easier for the visually impaired to read, it provides more information, in greater specificity, on accessibility (e.g., location of curbcuts, accessible features for

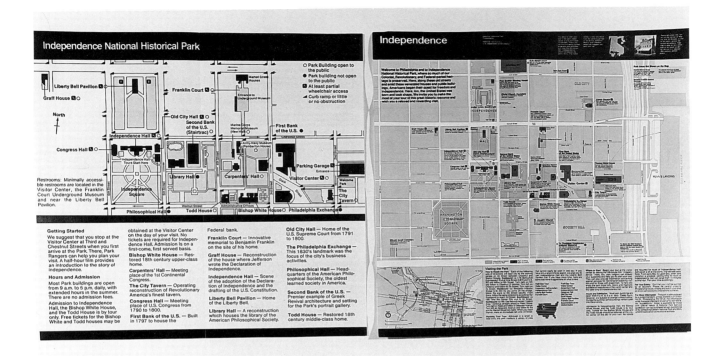

FIGURE 14.1
Map side of the two Independence National Historical Park brochures, Accessibility brochure is on the left.

hearing or sight impaired, and means of accessible entry) than the other brochure (Figure 14.1). The Accessibility brochure states:

> Independence National Historical Park poses challenging accessibility problems. Most of the buildings within the Park were constructed over two hundred years ago, and the National Park Service is responsible for maintaining them in their original condition. Since creating total physical accessibility would destroy the historic character of some of these structures, the Park is striving to provide alternate access through interpretive programs. At the same time, the Park is trying to make all services and activities meet the needs of those with physical impairments.

For buildings with only accessible first floors (by means of temporary ramp), the Park Service has photographic albums showing the upper floors. The two 1970s Park Service buildings, the Visitor Center and the Liberty Bell Pavilion, are accessible to someone in a wheelchair and offer exhibits on the site and buildings. To improve services for visitors with disabilities, a text telephone, lowered counter, and a new chart listing accessibility features have been added to the Visitor Center. For each building, the chart lists the accessibility features by disability category. For example, for the Visitor Center, under *Hearing Impairment* the chart states "tdd, phonic earphones for movie/house torus, captioned movie, scripts of movie." The large posted chart makes it easy and convenient for a visitor with a disability to find out *precisely* what accessibility modifications have been made. It is not sufficient to have accessible features. Their availability needs to be effectively communicated to the visitor, as has been done by the National Park Service at Independence National Historical Park. (For the visitor who is blind and unaccompanied, an audio announcement of accessibility features is also needed.)

Restrained by the architectural and historical importance of Independence Hall and the other nearby eighteenth-century buildings, which were restored prior to the 1960s, before accessibility was an issue, the Park Service emphasizes providing access through information. Photo albums show inaccessible spaces; amplification, captioning, and printed scripts improve communication for the hearing impaired; and tactile materials (models, maps, and reproductions of eighteenth-century furnishings) and detailed verbal descriptions by rangers help the visually impaired and blind understand the site. The accessibility brochure and the new chart assure that accessibility features can be found (the visitor who is blind still depends on someone to read the chart or brochure to find the accessibility information).

Independence National Historical Park also employs several people with disabilities as interpreters and maintenance workers. One interpreter who is visually impaired acts as an in-house consultant, checking text legibility, giving accessibility training to other employees, and answering questions they would feel uncomfortable asking of a visually impaired or blind outsider.

The National Park Service considers the recently restored Statue of Liberty, on Liberty Island, which reopened for its centennial in 1990, "a model of accessibility" although only those who can climb can get to the crown. Everything, except the statue, from the grounds to the museum in the pedestal of the statue has been made

FIGURE 14.2
Scale, tactile model of Liberty Island.

physically accessible. The paths from the boat to the statue are wide, firm, and level; accessible ramps, ticket windows, drinking fountains, bathrooms, concession areas, and telephones have been added. The elevator, with raised letters on the panel stops at each level in the pedestal. Large type signs, tactile models, accessibility brochures, captioned movies, and detailed audio tours serve the visually or hearing impaired (Figures 14.2 and 14.3). The most impressive accessible features in the museum are the full size reproductions of the face, foot, and armature of the statue, which museum visitors can touch (Figure 14.4). The National Park Service can justifiably argue that the restored Statue of Liberty (Blaine Cliver, AIA, NPS project manager; Swanke Hayden Connell restoration architects, and MetaForm, exhibit designer) is a model of accessibility with its enhanced accessibility of the grounds and museum, full-scale reproductions, and the 8-minute video that duplicates the climb to the crown of the statue, providing the experience for the person unable or unwilling to do it.

On Ellis Island, the attractive, restored facade of the main administration building of 1900, by Boring & Tilton, is nearly over-

FIGURE 14.3
Scale, tactile model of the Statue of Liberty.

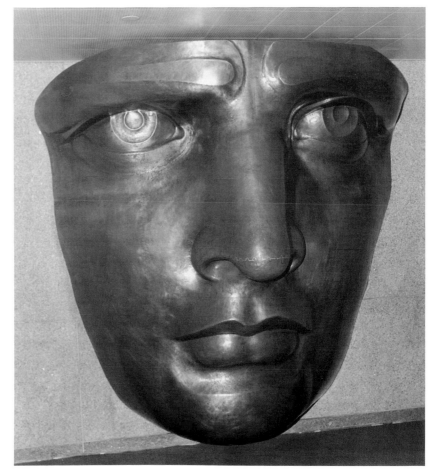

FIGURE 14.4
Full-size reproduction of the face of the Statue of Liberty.

shadowed by its 1980s stridently modern metal and glass canopy, by restoration architects Beyer Blinder Belle/Notter Finegold & Alexander. (Exhibits design by MetaForm; Michael Adlerstein, AIA, was National Park Service project manager.) The dramatic canopy covers the accessible ramp, flanked by stairs, that leads directly to the building's main entrance. (The canopy also articulates the Park Service's current philosophy of preferring "honest" contemporary design statements to "fake" restorations.) The boldness and placement of the ramp and its canopy state categorically that the restored Ellis Island main building is equally accessible to people with mobility impairments (Figure 14.5). (A second ramp on the side of the building leads to the food concession area.)

Wheelchair accessibility extends to the building's interior, where the information desk with lowered counter was built, elevators and ramps were installed, and accessible bathrooms (single and unisex) were created (Figure 14.6). In the historic bathrooms, in addition to a wide stall with grab bars, one sink has clear knee space with recessed drain pipes, lever handles, a mirror angled out from the top so that someone in a wheelchair can look up to the mirror and see him or herself, and a lowered paper dispenser (Figure 14.7). At

FIGURE 14.5
Ramp, stairs, and canopy at the entrance to Ellis Island main building.

FIGURE 14.6
Wheelchair-accessible middle portion of the information desk at Ellis Island.

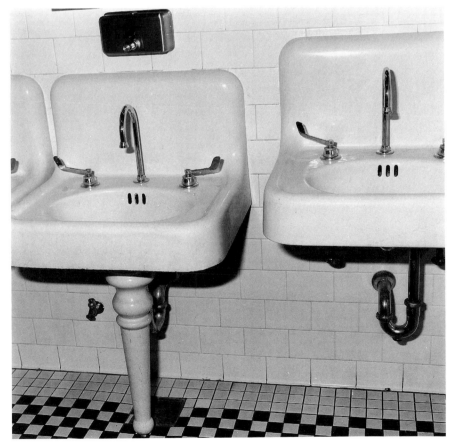

FIGURE 14.7
Ellis Island bathroom, with accessible sink (with recessed pipe) and angled mirror (not in photograph) to the right with inaccessible sink (pipe not recessed, leg blocking access) to left. Both sinks have accessible lever handles.

the top of the stairs, evacuation chairs are stored. With these chairs the rangers can wheel people down stairs with dignity instead of carrying them and without the rangers hurting themselves. (These chairs are also available at the Statue of Liberty.)

At Ellis Island, the National Park Service offers the same type of communication aids as at Independence Park and the Statue of Liberty to assure that people with either hearing or visual disabilities have access to all the information provided by the Park Service interpreters, movies, displays, and exhibits.

Liberty and Ellis Islands can only be reached by concessionaire ferry from lower Manhattan or New Jersey. The ferries are considered accessible because they have wheelchair tie downs to keep the chairs in place and the crew help people on the ramp. However, the ramp is steep and the gap between the ramp and the boat is wide (Figure 14.8). The National Park Service insists that concessionaires at park facilities be accessible and the concessionaires' efforts to improve accessibility are evaluated when concessionaire leases are renegotiated.

The bicentennial of the Declaration of Independence and the centennial restorations of Ellis Island and the Statue of Liberty have focused attention on the National Park Service's cultural holdings and their accessibility. But the Service is the guardian of equally important natural resources such as Yosemite National Park. The National Park Service has worked with the Department of Agriculture's Forest Service to write specific accessibility guide-

FIGURE 14.8
Steep ferry ramp at Ellis Island. The large gap between the boat and the ramp is not visible from this view.

lines for natural areas under federal control. The *Design Guide for Accessible Outdoor Recreation,* training sessions, movies, slide shows, and other National Park Service and Forest Service joint undertakings provide much more specific guidance for natural and recreational areas than the Uniform Federal Accessibility Standards or the ADA accessibility guidelines.

Despite shared symbolism and management, the Statue of Liberty, Ellis Island, and Independence Park are very different cultural landmarks. Independence Park, as an ensemble of restored eighteenth-century buildings and furnishings, is treated by the National Park Service as an architectural relic with too much integrity and significance to be permanently altered to provide physical accessibility. There, the Park Service's greatest and most successful accessibility efforts have been in providing clear, helpful information on what accessibility features exist. Independence's accessibility brochure is exemplary for its clarity and usefulness for visitors. And through the accessible Visitor Center, accessible Liberty Bell pavilion, the accessible first floors of some historic buildings, and the assistance of park rangers, literature, photographic albums, and captioned movies, the Park Service conveys a good sense of the inaccessible spaces, the events that occurred there, and the people who participated.

The Statue of Liberty by Frederic Auguste Bartholdi could not be made physically accessible without destroying it as an engineering and aesthetic statement. The pedestal was designed by Richard Morris Hunt, the dean of nineteenth-century American architects, and therefore has its own architectural importance, so it could not be changed on the exterior. Therefore, the Park Service concentrated its efforts on making the grounds and the museum in the pedestal physically and informationally accessible. A video of the climb to the top of the Statue makes that experience accessible to those with mobility disabilities. The scaled reproductions of the statue make the experience accessible for those with visual disabilities. For visitors with hearing impairments, captioned movies supplement the other visual information available.

At Ellis Island, in contrast to the Statue of Liberty and Independence Park, the Park Service has assertively made the building physically accessible. (That accessibility is complemented by the same information on accessibility used at the Statue of Liberty and Independence Park.) Clearly, the Park Service determined that the architectural significance of the slightly less than 100-year-old Ellis Island main building was less than that of the nearly 200-year-old (at time of restoration) Independence Park buildings and less than the architectural and engineering significance of the 100-year-old Statue of Liberty and its pedestal. But the Park Service's actions also signal that its pendulum is shifting from preservation to accessibility. The canopy at Ellis Island suggests that accessibility is sometimes more important than an exact restoration. (The Park Service said it had sufficient historic documentation to exactly duplicate the original canopy if it had wanted to do so.)

By having a well-thought-out policy on accessibility, the Park Service does not lose sight of its goal of providing equal, but not separate, accessibility to people with disabilities and the non-disabled. Yet it remains flexible enough to tailor its accessibility features to the specific significance of the resource and to tailor its preservation efforts to the specific accessibility needs of the resource.

Chapter 15

HISTORICAL SOCIETY OF WASHINGTON

Washington, D.C.'s best known monuments sit in lush green expanses, but some of the city's most interesting buildings occupy the oddly shaped lots created by Pierre Charles L'Enfant's 1791 plan. Upon the north-south and east-west grid of streets the French engineer imposed wide diagonal avenues to link monuments such as the United States Capitol and the President's House, creating truncated parcels. A century later, another immigrant built one of the best houses on one of L'Enfant's difficult lots. In 1892–1894, northwest of the White House and just below the monumental Dupont Circle, German-American brewmaster Christian Heurich built his mansion (Figure 15.1). Heurich's architect, John Granville Meyers, anchored the house with a prominent capped tower at the corner where New Hampshire Avenue intersects 19th Street and Sunderland Place. On the main facade facing the avenue, Meyers placed a massive porte-cochere. The corner tower and main facade are faced in brownstone while the secondary facade along Sunderland and the rear garden facades are brick. This late Richardsonian mansion's mixture of treatments and materials—bold tower and porte-cochere, rough hewn sandstone and smooth subdued brick—perfectly matches the lot's shape and location.

The Heurich mansion's interior is an equally powerful expression of late nineteenth-century taste, climaxing in a dramatic, overwhelming mahogany and oak dining room. Heurich lived amid this ornate splendor until his death at age 102 in 1945. His widow subsequently donated the house to the Columbia Historical Society (now the Historical Society of Washington, D.C.), which has occupied it since 1956.

In the late 1970s the Society raised money to make the house museum accessible. A lift was to replace the cast-iron stairs behind the house, leading from the street to the garden. A rear door opening onto the garden was to provide access to the first floor of the house and an interior elevator was to be installed in the original,

FIGURE 15.1
Historical Society of Washington, D.C.

but never used, elevator shaft to provide accessibility to the upper floors. Such a route, starting at the rear of the house, would have struck present-day users as second class access, but the Society's primary concern was to provide access without altering the major facades.

Once the Society's architect, Geier Brown Renfrow, prepared plans for the elevator mechanism it become apparent that only an inadequately small elevator cab would fit in the original shaft (Figure 15.2). Also, a National Park Service historical architect recommended against using the existing elevator shaft because inserting the needed machinery would damage the interior's historic fabric. These problems, coupled with changes in the Society's board and staff, resulted in the Society scrapping the proposed garden lift and interior elevator.

A five-story elevator shaft along the north party wall was erected in 1988 at a cost of $350,000—with most of the funding from a National Endowment for the Humanities grant. According to project architect, Baird Smith, AIA, the major cost was for the custom elevator with doors on three sides. At street level, the exterior elevator doors open on the west; in the basement, first, and second floors they open on the east; and on the third and fourth floors they open on the south. On the two upper floors the elevator door frame was built into an undecorated wall next to the fireplace; in the basement the frame was cut into a storeroom wall. At the first and second floors, the elevator opens onto a landing and a door (originally a window) into the office wing (Figure 15.3). The elevator was added without changing important walls or spaces, and at the first and second floors the transition from elevator to mansion is so natural that most visitors probably assume the elevator is original.

More discerning visitors see the elevator structure as a sensitive addition to the mansion. The water table, decorative raised panel, and arch of the elevator housing relate it to the original building, but the elevator's different color brick indicates it was built later

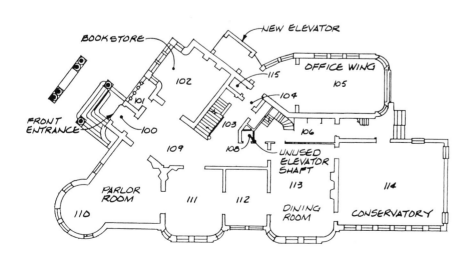

FIGURE 15.2
First floor plan. (From EA-Mueller, Inc., Consulting Engineers, 1989. Reproduced by permission of EA-Mueller.)

FIGURE 15.3
First floor elevator landing and window lengthened into door, viewed from the office wing.

(Figure 15.4) The architect added enough details to the elevator block to assure that it is compatible, without making it into a fake nineteenth-century elevator housing (Figure 15.5).

The Heurich Mansion demonstrates the architectural truth that challenged architects create better designs. L'Enfant's 1791 street plan challenged Heurich's architect a century later. Meyers responded with a gusty building equal to its prominent, but difficult lot. He, in turn, challenged the Society and its architect, nearly a hundred years later, to overcome the allure of the existing elevator shaft and to provide accessibility without damaging the pristine Victorian interiors. Suitably modest and cleverly related, the Society's elevator is the ideal companion to L'Enfant's lot and Heurich's mansion.

FIGURE 15.4
Elevator with closed-circuit monitor on wall to right.

FIGURE 15.5
Elevator housing viewed from north.

107

Section VI

PUBLIC ACCOMMODATIONS

The Americans with Disabilities Act requires previously exempt (under federal law) public accommodations to become accessible. Not all public accommodations waited for the threat of a federal lawsuit to act. Whether motivated by a sense of equality, personal experience, religious conviction, or a desire to tap new markets, the managers of the public accommodations discussed in this section made their facilities accessible before the passage of ADA. Why or when they became accessible, however, is less important than their management's attitude toward their accessible service:

1. It is not static, but evolutionary.
2. It is experimental, and various solutions must be tried and evaluated.
3. It goes well beyond the removal of physical barriers.
4. It uses new technologies where appropriate.
5. It does not make assumptions about the capability and needs of a patron with disabilities.
6. It requires proper training and personnel manuals.
7. Only people with disabilities can ultimately evaluate accessibility.

Public accommodations vary in their reasons for being accessible, their degree of accessibility, and which disabilities they accommodate, but collectively—through words and actions—they, of all accessible buildings, best convey the issues involved in accessible design.

Washington, D.C.'s Arena Stage is a recognized leader in making live theater accessible. By using innovative accessibility techniques and technologies, several of which it invented, the Arena has expanded its audience to include people who use wheelchairs, have limited hearing or sight, or who are blind or deaf. Other theaters such as the Shakespeare Theatre, also in Washington, share the Arena's desire to reach the largest audience and have incorporated some of the Arena's accessibility methods. Because the Shakespeare is newer, it offers better accessibility for patrons in wheelchairs than the Arena does. (The Paper Mill Playhouse in Millburn, NJ, which offers extensive physical, visual, and auditory accessibility features—including a pre-performance tour of the stage for people who are blind or have limited vision where they can touch the props, costumes, and scenery to get a sense of the play—is considered by some to be the most accessible live theater.) The Arena deserves credit for its commitment to and innovations in accessibility and its willingness to share its experience in the field. But the Arena deserves at least as much credit for the section in its personnel manual on the needs of patrons with disabilities. The staff are instructed to inform patrons specifically as to what services are available and to inquire if any services are needed. They are told not to assume what, if any, services are wanted, and to treat all patrons respectfully.

The Cheesecake Factory restaurant, in upper northwest Washington, D.C. also has an excellent personnel manual with a section on serving patrons with disabilities. The section is based largely on the National Easter Seal's publications. It emphasizes the proper language to be used and the attitude to be shown toward people with disabilities. It also details what needs such patrons might have; however it clearly states that the patron must decide what, if any, accommodations are needed and if they are satisfactory.

A nationally prominent museum director who uses a wheelchair assumes that when she travels, which is frequently, that she will not be able to use the hotel shower. If she were to stay at the newer Hyatts she would find roll-in showers and several other accessible features in designated rooms. Also, if she arrived at Baltimore Washington International Airport rather than the Capitol's other two, larger airports, she would see accessible, unisex bathrooms and other features especially helpful to hearing impaired and deaf travelers. (Portland, Oregon's International Airport proposes to install two-way emergency communications, talking signs, wayfarer finders, and other technologies that will substantially advance airport accessibility.)

The National Wildlife Federation maintains nature trails, including an accessible one, to educate Americans to the beauty and importance of preserving the natural habitat. Not only does the Federation's Mountain Laurel Trail in Vienna, Virginia, demonstrate accessible, multisensory nature exploration, but the process of planning for the trail (and now for its expansion) is a model of how to design accessible facilities.

(At the opposite end of outdoor environments—not in terms of services, but of setting—is Longwood Gardens in Wilmington, DE. With its formal beauty of well-trimmed lawns and architecturally elegant flower house, this early-twentieth-century DuPont property has had limited retrofittings to make it more accessible. In its flower house, the stairs have been ramped and elevators take patrons to the accessible basement bathrooms. Also, the wide, smooth walkways through the more level grounds have been marked as accessible

FIGURE VI.1
*Longwood Gardens, Wilmington, DE. Two
people in wheelchairs rolling away from and
one person with a cane walking toward the
photographer. Notice the flatness and width
of path, although benches are not recessed.*

FIGURE VI.2
*Longwood Gardens, Wilmington, DE.
Signage indicating accessible path.*

(Figures IV.1 and IV.2). Closer in resemblance to the National Wildlife
Federation's accessible trail is Buttonbush Trail at Cape Cod National
Seashore, where the National Park Service has installed guide ropes and
braille and large-print signs describing the plantings and animals along
the path. Every year since its creation in 1970, students at the Perkins
School for the Blind, among others, both disabled and nondisabled,
have walked this trail.

Orioles Park at Camden Yards had immediate acceptance by fans
and players for its old-fashioned ambiance. In the next few years, no
doubt, designers of new baseball and football stadiums will try to
replicate its comforting nostalgia. But its comprehensive planning for
and subtle implementation of accessibility features, especially its highly
original accessible seating, will be Oriole Park's legacy.

Much less expensive and emphasizing participatory rather than
spectator recreation is the accessible Chinn Aquatics & Fitness Center
in northern Virginia. The center is the successful expression of a local
government's commitment to provide much more than the minimally
required accessible exercise programs and facility, by an architect able
to attractively integrate accessibility into the design of the building and
its park setting.

The only public accommodations exempt from the Americans with
Disabilities Act are private clubs and religious institutions. Still covered

by local building code requirements for accessibility, churches and synagogues at least are starting to provide a ramped approach, but often not at the main entrance. St. Elizabeth and Baltimore Hebrew establish a higher accessible (and moral) standard for religious buildings to emulate.

Charleston's Waterfront Park, a most ambitious and successful design, reflects 30 years of a prominent landscape architect's efforts to create aesthetically pleasing, vibrant urban scenes experienced on accessible paths. Its use of gravel, and the relationship between the steps and ramps will not please all, but the park makes a thoughtful, compelling argument for its particular use of these elements.

David Andrews, Program Manager, Information Access Project for Blind Individuals, National Federation of the Blind, was one of the disability advocates who was asked in early 1992 by the Baltimore Washington International Airport to evaluate its compliance with the ADA accessibility guidelines. Andrews's recommendations to the airport apply to all public accommodations and graphically express the importance of the vendor's attitude toward providing accessible service to patrons with disabilities:

> The ADA requires that public facilities, such as BWI Airport, offer disabled persons accommodations. There is, however a further provision in the Act, originally sponsored by the National Federation of the Blind, which says that a disabled person has the right to refuse any accommodation offered. While this may seem to be a trivial matter to some persons, it is not always. Most blind people who have traveled at all have had the experience of airline personnel insisting that we ride in the motorized electric carts many of them use. Most blind persons have no problem walking, and the use of such carts is unnecessary at best and demeaning at worst. While we do not want to preclude their use by others, we do not want to be coerced to use an "accommodation" which we do not want and/or need. The use of any accommodation has to be under the control of the individual potentially using it, not the provider. Workshops can educate your personnel about this and other matters.
>
> Blind people, and all people for that matter, vary in their abilities and training. For example, most blind people can travel freely and independently using a long white cane or guide dog. However, some others may require more sighted assistance. Your personnel need to be sensitized to our varying abilities and needs.
>
> Another bone of contention among blind persons concerns the use of the metal scanners at the security check points. Some airport personnel insist on taking our canes from us, under the belief that they are metal and will set off the equipment. While some canes are made of aluminum and/or other metals, most are made of fiberglass or other nonferrous materials. It is much easier to go through the scanning arch with a cane. While we do not want to impede the security check process, we also feel that we have the right to use our mobility tools to achieve the greatest degree of independence and freedom possible.

Some people in wheelchairs, by contrast, complain of perfunctory inspections at airport security gates. The guards, apparently afraid of contracting a disability, do not check the person in the chair or the chair for concealed weapons. An inappropriate attitude replaces architectural barriers with equally demeaning behavioral barriers.

Removing physical barriers is only one part of accessibility. Applying new technologies, inventing new architectural features (such as accessible seats), designing spaces capable of accommodating these new architectural and technological elements, and properly training personnel, done with input at all phases from people with disabilities, are needed for public accommodations to serve larger, more diverse audiences.

Chapter 16

ARENA STAGE AND SHAKESPEARE THEATRE

A few months after Title III of the Americans with Disabilities Act went into effect on January 26, 1992, *The New York Times* ran two brief essays poignantly conveying the personal anguish of people in wheelchairs who attend or try to attend inaccessible New York City theaters, managed by people insensitive to the needs and rights of the patrons. Robert C. Samuels wrote, in June, " . . . Go see *The Waterdance*. You'll learn how it feels to face life in a wheelchair, but you won't find out what it's like to live in one unless you try to do something difficult, something like rolling into a New York movie house." In April, TV journalist John Hockenberry recounted his efforts to go to another theater:

> "You are a fire hazard, sir," the manager insisted. Only moments before I had been a component of his cash flow. I grabbed his collar and told him what he could do with his Policy for Disabled Patrons. I was easily over-powered and ushered, the only ushering I would experience that night, to the 52nd Street Sidewalk. I sat powerless and humiliated; all dressed up, nowhere to go . . . [I]t seemed as if I was the only one who thought that a few stairs shouldn't stand in the way of seeing a play.

If Hockenberry and Samuels were to attend Washington, D.C.'s Arena Stage or Shakespeare Theatre at the Lansburgh, they would have dramatically better experiences. The Arena Stage's enlightened and committed management has for nearly 15 years devised inno-vative solutions to make its plays more accessible to patrons, re-gardless of their disability. The Shakespeare Theatre, in a brand-new facility, has avoided most of the physical barriers of the Arena while borrowing the new assistive technologies used (and often pioneered) at the Arena.

The Arena Stage complex, designed by Harry Weese and built in two phases in the 1960s, consists of the original Arena Stage, an 800-seat theater-in-the-round; the Kreeger Theater, a 500-seat thrust theater; and the Old Vat, originally a rehearsal hall which

FIGURE 16.1
Arena Stage theater in foreground, entrance
lobby in rear to the right.

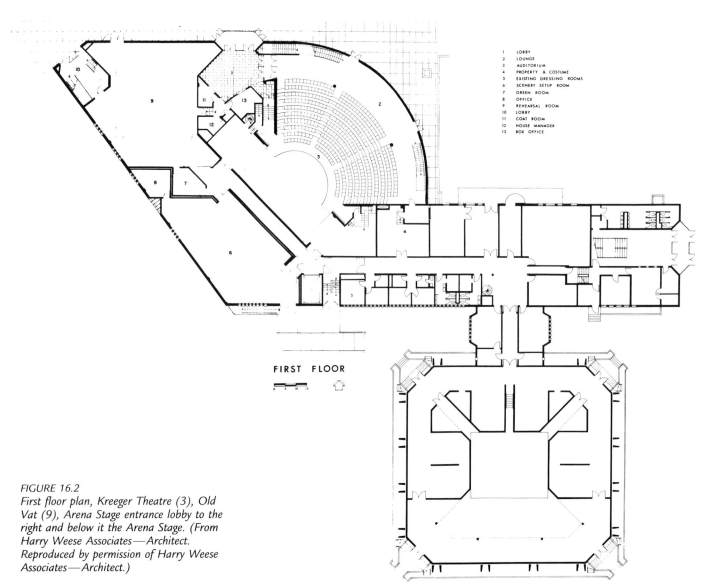

1   LOBBY
2   LOUNGE
3   AUDITORIUM
4   PROPERTY & COSTUME
5   EXISTING DRESSING ROOMS
6   SCENERY SETUP ROOM
7   GREEN ROOM
8   OFFICE
9   REHEARSAL ROOM
10 LOBBY
11 COAT ROOM
12 HOUSE MANAGER
13 BOX OFFICE

FIRST FLOOR

FIGURE 16.2
First floor plan, Kreeger Theatre (3), Old
Vat (9), Arena Stage entrance lobby to the
right and below it the Arena Stage. (From
Harry Weese Associates—Architect.
Reproduced by permission of Harry Weese
Associates—Architect.)

116

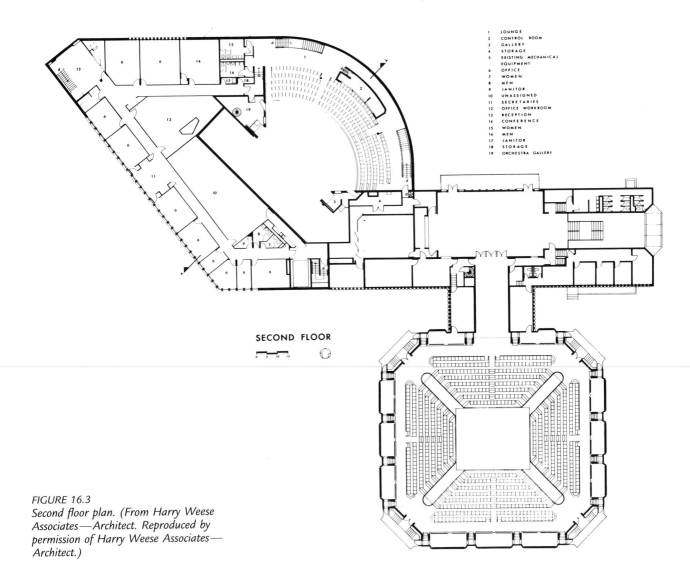

1   LOUNGE
2   CONTROL ROOM
3   GALLERY
4   STORAGE
5   EXISTING MECHANICAL
    EQUIPMENT
6   OFFICE
7   WOMEN
8   MEN
9   JANITOR
10 UNASSIGNED
11 SECRETARIES
12 OFFICE WORKROOM
13 RECEPTION
14 CONFERENCE
15 WOMEN
16 MEN
17 JANITOR
18 STORAGE
19 ORCHESTRA GALLERY

SECOND FLOOR

0   5   10   15

FIGURE 16.3
Second floor plan. (From Harry Weese
Associates—Architect. Reproduced by
permission of Harry Weese Associates—
Architect.)

seats up to 180 (Figures 16.1, 16.2, and 16.3). As built, the Arena
Stage made no provision for patrons with mobility or other disabil-
ities; the lobby to the Arena has stairs and both the Kreeger and
Arena have steps in the aisles and fixed seating.

The Arena's first formal efforts to accommodate people with
disabilities were made in 1979. It introduced sign language interpretation for certain performances and solicited people to serve on
an "advisory council on problems related to the handicapped." The
next year, grab bars were added in the bathrooms and a chair lift
was installed in the lobby (Figure 16.4). Prior to the lift, the staff
carried people with mobility impairments up and down the stairs.

In 1981 and 1982, the Arena added sound amplification for the
hearing impaired and (for certain performances) audio description
for the visually impaired, both through headsets. Program books in
large print, in braille, or on cassette are now available, and a play
synopsis can be borrowed in advance of the performance. Tickets
can be ordered by text telephone and text telephones will be placed

FIGURE 16.4
Chair lift in the entrance lobby of Arena Stage.

in the lobby enabling people attending the theater to make outgoing calls. The Arena is also investigating the possible use for hearing impaired or deaf patrons of laptop computers displaying dialogue. The only patron parking is for people with mobility disabilities.

The Arena's original advisory committee of people with disabilities has grown into several committees, each representing a specific type of disability. In addition, other people with disabilities, such as Price Baum (see Chapter 10 on National Rehabilitation Hospital) informally advise the Arena. Perhaps most important, a college student with a disability is an intern working with the Arena's access director (Figure 16.5). The Arena does not assume it can anticipate the needs of people with disabilities; they are actively involved in helping the Arena identify and solve accessibility problems.

The Arena, in turn, properly trains its staff to enhance accessibility. All Arena employees are expected to be prepared and sensitive to the particular needs of patrons with disabilities, whether it is the manager who operates the stair lift, the parking attendant who makes sure the patron in a wheelchair is directed to the accessible stage door entrance rather than the inaccessible front entrance of the Old Vat, or the telephone operator who is instructed not to

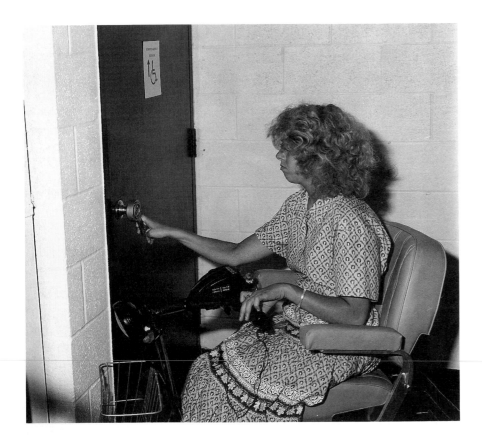

FIGURE 16.5
Jeri Esocoff Zimmerman, an intern in the Arena Stage's access office has angled her cart so that she can reach the handle and still open the door without her cart blocking it. A lever handle has been fitted over the round knob, and signs indicating the route to the accessible bathroom have been added.

assume what services a disabled person ordering tickets will need, but to tell him or her what services are available.

The Arena's staff access manual is a model for thoughtful, detailed instructions (e.g., identifying which seats in each theater are best for a patron who can transfer from a wheelchair) and for the attitude it wants to instill in employees. "The first contact the public has with the staff at Arena Stage sets the tone for how the individual perceives the theater and what type of experience it is going to be. This booklet was put together to help the process of establishing a positive and assistive relationship between the patron who has extra needs due to a disability and Arena Stage."

Even a skilled staff cannot completely overcome the physical barriers of the Arena's two theaters with fixed seating and stepped aisles. Like other theaters, it places people in wheelchairs who cannot transfer to theater seats at the ends of some aisles, above the vom (a ramp to the stage), and behind the last row (probably violating fire codes) (Figure 16.6). But unlike other theaters, the Arena places a seat next to the wheelchair behind the last row for the person's companion, and does not sell tickets for the two seats in front of them. Other theaters separate the person in the wheelchair and his or her companion. (Whether most theaters leave empty the seat in front of the person in the wheelchair is not known.) By seating the person in the wheelchair with his or her companion, the Arena shows a sensitivity that is lacking in other theaters' management.

FIGURE 16.6
Wheelchair seating at the end of the last row in the Arena Stage.

The Arena is, at present, experimenting with possible permanent seating options for people in wheelchairs. One of the tiers in the original Arena Stage is of wooden construction, rather than concrete, so the Arena can now remove seats in the wooden tier and try various wheelchair seating options. When it finds the best one, it will install it permanently. (The theater was built with a wooden tier to give the Arena the option of removing that tier and converting the theater in the round to a thrust theater.)

The assistive technologies used, sometimes for the first time anywhere, at the Arena Stage are, to varying degrees, now available in other theaters. The Shakespeare Theatre at the Lansburgh, for example, offers sign interpretation or audio description at selected performances, has sound amplification, and braille, large print and audio cassette programs.

Designed by Graham Gund Architects (Bill Erickson, project architect) and developed by its sister company, Gunwyn (Peter Madsen, FAIA, is president of Gunwyn and managing principal of Graham Gund Architects), the Lansburgh is an approximately 700,00-square-foot in-fill, mixed-use building on Washington, D.C.'s 7th Street, the city's old retail corridor and now its arts corridor (Figure 16.7). Since The Shakespeare Theatre at the Lansburgh is a new theater (opened in March 1992) in a new building, it was built

FIGURE 16.7
Shakespeare Theatre at the Lansburgh.

without most of the physical barriers of the Arena Stage. The theater's entrance is level with the sidewalk, the foyer's ticket window and pay telephones are lowered, and the bathrooms (conveniently located) adjacent to the lobby have accessible toilets and sinks.

The theater's most important accessibility feature is its last row of movable chairs (Figure 16.8). A chair is removed to provide space for a person in a wheelchair and his or her companion sits in the adjacent seat. This is an imperfect solution because it limits people in wheelchairs to the last row, but it is still a great improvement over seating people in wheelchairs in an aisle or in the passageway behind the last row. It is also more economical than permanently removing a certain number of seats to provide wheelchair space that will not always be used. And it is more flexible than requiring a patron in a wheelchair to reserve a seat in advance and then unbolting and removing a seat to provide wheelchair space for that

FIGURE 16.8
Removable chairs in the last row.

FIGURE 16.9
Site plan. 7th Street entrance for parking
garage elevator is next to retail space 1.
(From The Gunwyn Company, developer,
and Graham Gund Architects, Inc.,
architect. Reproduced by permission of The
Gunwyn Company.)

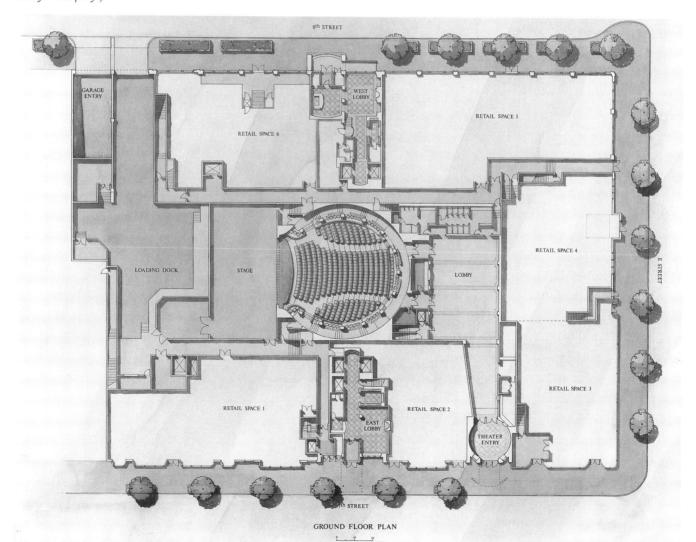

GROUND FLOOR PLAN

performance. Another feature of the Shakespeare Theatre that benefits patrons with mobility impairments is the compact layout of the lobby, foyer, bathrooms, and theater, reducing the distance a patron has to walk or roll (Figure 16.9).

In the theater's second performance one of the roles was played by an actor who used a wheelchair. An elevator, exclusively for people with mobility impairments, took him from the entrance lobby to the changing rooms one floor below. There, the changing rooms and bathrooms were accessible, and—most impressive—one shower was a roll-in and the other had a transfer seat. (Both showers should have handheld shower heads and relocated controls, and the transfer shower should not have a high sill.) From the changing room, the actor took a chair lift to the rear of the stage. Peter Madsen, FAIA, of Graham Gund Architects and Gunwyn, believes the Shakespeare Theatre offers the best access to the stage for an actor in a wheelchair of any theater he has seen (Figure 16.10).

Reserved parking for people with disabilities is provided in the building's underground garage, but its street entrance is a few store

FIGURE 16.10
Stair lift from actors' changing rooms to backstage.

FIGURE 16.11 Parking garage's accessible ramp to elevator.

ELEVATOR
TO THEATRE
TO 7th STREET

fronts from the theater entrance, requiring people to travel outside between the garage and the theater (Figure 16.9). Also, the wider parking spaces for disabled drivers are not always adjacent to the ramp to the elevator (Figure 16.11).

The Arena Stage and the Shakespeare Theatre, unlike other institutions, strive to be accessible to all people with disabilities rather than only a particular segment of the population with disabilities—usually people in wheelchairs. This inclusive approach to accessibility grows out of these theaters' educational goals. "Accessibility programming at Arena Stage," according to its access director Martha Ingel, "is not a priority because of the law, but springs from a deep desire to reach all audiences with our artistic message." Such an attitude helps assure that the staff are sensitive and trained to assist people, to the degree they desire help, and such a commitment drives the Arena's continual enhancement of its accessibility features. The Shakespeare Theatre has been able to build on the experience of the Arena, effectively using assistive technology, avoiding major physical barriers, and making significant improvements in physical accessibility for patrons and employees. But some remaining barriers (e.g., stepped aisles and the location of accessible seating)—created at least in part by structural and fiscal restraints—await innovative design solutions.

Chapter 17

ORIOLES PARK AT CAMDEN YARDS

The Orioles' new stadium in Baltimore opened for the 1992 baseball season to nearly universal praise. The National Organization on Disability (N.O.D.) commended the Orioles, the Maryland Stadium Authority, and Maryland Governor William Donald Schaefer for designing and building a "fully accessible" ballpark. A N.O.D. official said that "While the Americans With Disabilities Act requires accessible public facilities, this action demonstrates the spirit and not just the letter of the law." The American Institute of Architects honored the Maryland Stadium Authority and its designers (HOK Sports Facilities Group [architect of record], RTKL Associates, Inc., and Wallace, Roberts & Todd) with an Urban Design Excellence Award. One of seven projects recognized out of 138 considered in this new AIA awards program, the authority's master plan "successfully merges large-scale use into an established urban fabric." Architectural critics were equally impressed with the stadium's detailing, massing, and compatibility with its surroundings. Even the baseball fans, players, and sports writers praised the park—for its old-fashioned intimacy and irregular layout, reminiscent of early-twentieth-century downtown ballparks. It is rare for a design to satisfy such a diverse group of critics, and it is even rarer for such a revolutionary design—in terms of accessibility—to evoke nostalgia.

The most innovative and potentially influential accessibility feature at Orioles Park is the "equal access seat." It is a permanent seat cantilevered from a single vertical pole. The seat and armrests raise up and the entire unit pivots 90 degrees out of the way when someone in a wheelchair is sitting in the space. This flexible seating allows a person in a wheelchair to sit next to a companion not in a wheelchair or for two or more fans in wheelchairs to sit next to each other. The row of flexible seating and the aisle behind it are deep enough to allow a person with long legs to stretch out and still have people walk in the aisle (Figures 17.1 and 17.2).

FIGURE 17.1
Marian Vessels, Maryland governor's aide for ADA, sits in the lower deck equal access seating space. She is leaning on the chair that was pivoted out of the way to provide space for her wheelchair.

Approximately 1% of the stadium's 48,000 seats are wheelchair accessible and are in most sections of the park. Because people in wheelchairs would not be able to see when the fans in front stand, the row of accessible seating in the upper deck is elevated to provide an unobstructed view (except for the railing) even when people are standing (Figures 17.3 and 17.4). In addition to equal access seating in the upper and lower decks, a level platform, without chairs, for people in wheelchairs was built next to the press box, on the clubhouse level (Figure 17.5). In terms of cost of tickets and location (deck and side of stadium), people in wheelchairs have nearly the same choices as nondisabled fans.

Accessible seating is only as good as the accessible route to the seating, and Orioles Park has excellent accessible routes not only to the seats but to its other accessible features as well. Each level of the stadium has a wide promenade along which are the food concessions, accessible bathrooms, lowered drinking fountains and telephones, and the tunnels leading to the seating. At the end of the tunnel for the upper and lower deck are the accessible rows, so there are no stairs between the accessible seating and the route to them. The upper levels of the promenade are accessible by elevators placed throughout the park, or by the accessible ramps. Each ramp has a level platform at the beginning and end of each run and at every 30 feet along the run (Figure 17.6). The ramps, which are quite wide and offer panoramic views of Baltimore probably appeal

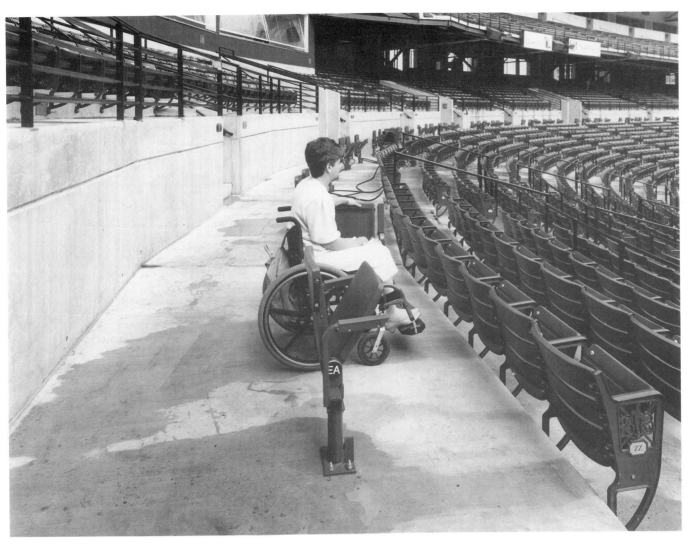

FIGURE 17.2
Adequate space provided in the aisle and in the equal access seat space for people to pass in the aisle even if the person in the wheelchair has very long legs. Side view of an equal access seat ready for a nondisabled patron.

FIGURE 17.3
Upper deck accessible seat is much higher than the row in front to provide an unobstructed view when fans stand.

FIGURE 17.4
Upper deck row of accessible seating
showing width of aisle. Seat in the
foreground has armrests and seat raised
and has been pivoted out of way.

FIGURE 17.5
View from upper deck toward home plate.
Upper and lower deck accessible seat are in
front of the tunnels. To the right of the
press box is the elevator and platform for a
group of fans in wheelchairs.

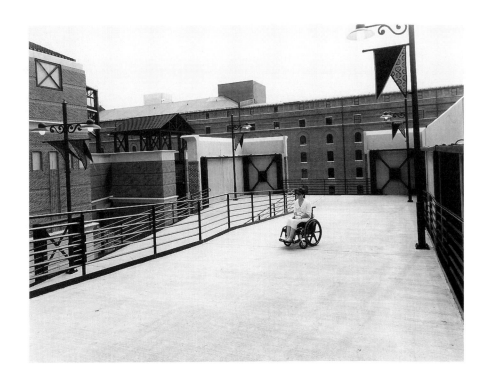

FIGURE 17.6
Marian Vessels at one of the level resting
platforms on each run of the accessible
ramp.

equally to all fans, nondisabled and in wheelchairs. Nothing about
the ramp suggests the stigma of "handicapped ramp." (An elevator
provides access to the platform for wheelchairs next to the press
box.) Advance ticket sales windows that have been lowered to be
accessible to someone in a wheelchair are located adjacent to the
accessible elevator on the upper deck promenade (see Figure 17.7).
The food concessions are accessible; they have lowered counter
tops, wide aisles, and lowered condiment tables (see Figure 17.8). In
addition to the promenade's accessible single-sex bathrooms, Orioles Park has two accessible unisex bathrooms in the first aid stations. Such bathrooms are invaluable for people who have attendants of the opposite sex or for a child who goes to the stadium
with an adult of the opposite sex. The first aid stations also offer
electrical outlets for recharging electric carts or wheelchairs.

The stadium's accessible routes start not in the stadium or at its
gates, but at the public transportation stops, adjacent parking lots,
and perimeter sidewalks. The light rail stops near the park are
elevated, making the trains accessible to someone with a mobility
disability (Figure 17.9). The 200 accessible parking spaces, 2% of the
total, are wide, clearly marked, and close to the Eutaw Street entrance to the park (Figure 17.10). Several of those spaces are on the
same side of the lot as the accessible ramp from the lot to the
walkway. Such spaces are preferable because it is dangerous for
people in wheelchairs to cross a parking lot; drivers backing up
have trouble seeing someone in a wheelchair. The Eutaw Street
entrance, like most of the entrances, does not have stairs. Those
entrances with stairs also have ramps (Figure 17.11). At all en-

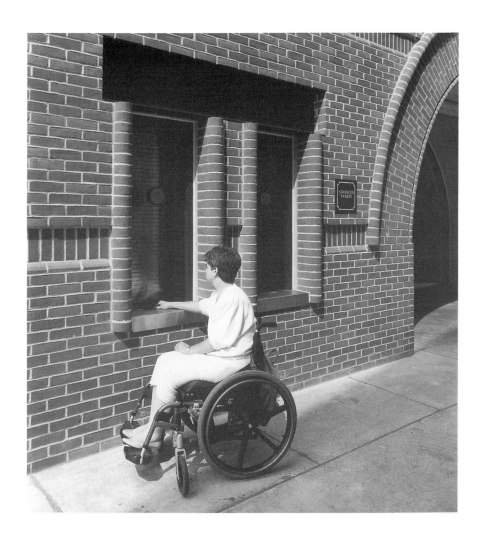

FIGURE 17.7
Lowered window sills at advanced ticket
window on the upper promenade. Elevator
is to the right.

FIGURE 17.8
Accessible condiment table in the foreground
and accessible concession stand at rear.

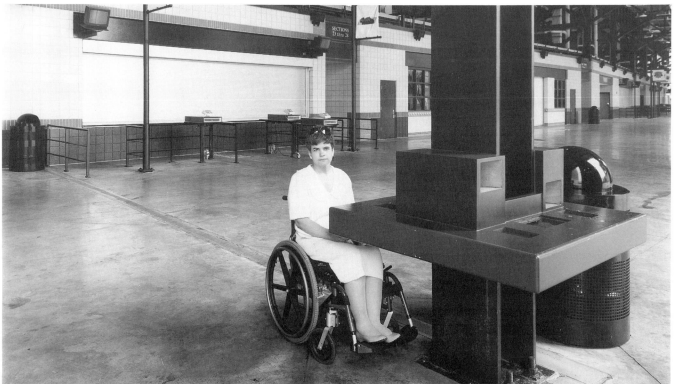

FIGURE 17.9
Accessible platform for light rail stop.

FIGURE 17.10
Some of the accessible parking closest to stadium. Ramp from the parking lot to the walkway is on the right. The walkway leads directly to the Eutaw Street gate.

trances, people in wheelchairs hand their tickets to the usher and wheel around instead of through the turnstile. Ticket sale windows at the entrances also have some lowered sills for people in wheelchairs or who are short. The major entrance to Orioles Park, the Eutaw Street gates, serves people coming from parking lots, public transportation or rolling/walking over from nearby hotels and convention facilities; the wide level walkways of Eutaw Street are not only accessible, but they are inviting urban spaces, which are quite rare in twentieth-century American cities (Figure 17.12).

FIGURE 17.11
Inside stadium entrance with stairs and accessible ramp to the right.

The emphasis at the Orioles Park is on wheelchair accessibility, but other means of accessibility also have been addressed:

- The signage is large.
- All audio announcements are also displayed on the giant screen in center field.
- Amplified versions of the announcements can be heard on headsets provided by the Orioles.
- Emergency alarms blink as well as sound.
- Tickets can be ordered by text telephone.
- For emergencies, text telephones are available to patrons.
- The Orioles have trained their ushers in basic sign language.
- An attractive booklet has been prepared describing accessible features.
- The ball club has hired people with disabilities. (In fact, when the stadium authority's contractors produced the prototype of the equal access seat, the Orioles had one of its part-time employees, who is in a wheelchair, test it.)

The equal access seat, like the ballpark's other accessible features, was an outgrowth of the Committee on Accessibility, appointed by the Maryland governor to advise the stadium authority and its architects. The governor's aide, Gertrude R. Jeffers, had the Committee meet with the Volunteers for Medical Engineering to conceptualize a wheelchair-accessible chair. The Volunteers is a nonprofit, Baltimore-based group of engineers who devise low-cost assistive technology to help people with disabilities. Kim Beasley, AIA (see Chapter 25), the sole architect on the accessibility committee, played a key role in conceiving the accessible seating and in

FIGURE 17.12
View from the walkway toward the ballpark, showing the wide, level walkways and the long urban plaza defined by the park on the left and the Camden Yards warehouse on the right. Gate C is closest to the accessible parking lots. Patrons who park in the north parking lots or east of the warehouse or who walk from downtown would enter at the far end of Gate A.

developing the "Accessibility Design Program for Baltimore Orioles Stadium." This detailed report, which guided the stadium authority, its architects, and the Orioles in addressing accessibility issues, reflected the expertise and experience of the members of the Committee and public input from the meetings held by the Committee around the state of Maryland.

It seems inevitable that other new parks will resemble Orioles Park at Camden Yards. Its colors, details, and general appearance create a "time stood still" ambience especially appropriate for the nation's pastime. It seems equally likely that the Orioles' highly successful, yet largely inconspicuous, equal access seating and other accessible features will be copied in other parks. The designers of new stadiums would also be well served to borrow Maryland's approach of involving people with disabilities and other disability experts starting at the earliest planning phase.

Chapter 18

ST. ELIZABETH AND BALTIMORE HEBREW

When Percival Goodman, FAIA (1904–1989), designed the Baltimore Hebrew synagogue in 1950, accessibility was clearly not a concern (Figure 18.1). Yet 40 years later, the state of Maryland honored the congregation for its recent improvements that made the synagogue accessible, or at least more accessible. In 1966, Dennis Madden (see Chapter 26) designed an accessible church for the smaller and less wealthy St. Elizabeth Roman Catholic congregation 35 miles south of Baltimore, in Rockville, Maryland, and this church has not needed any further accessibility changes since completion (Figure 18.2). A church and a synagogue—both built in

FIGURE 18.1
Baltimore Hebrew, main elevation.

FIGURE 18.2
St. Elizabeth, main elevation.

post–World War II modernist style, but with different approaches to accessibility—suggest the options open to designers or renovators of other religious buildings who have yet to address the issue.

The first pastor of St. Elizabeth, Reverend Frederick Bloom, instructed architect Madden to build the new church without steps. Having previously served an elderly congregation in a northwest Washington, D.C. church where the parishioners had to climb a dozen or more steep steps to enter the church, Bloom witnessed first-hand the problems created by architectural barriers. None of the five entrances to St. Elizabeth has steps, and all the entrances are only a short distance by level walkway from the parking lots to either side of the church. The parking spaces closest to the walkways are reserved for people with disabilities. Only the driveway in front of the church has a curb. But the parking lots are as close to the main entrance as the driveway, so no person with a mobility impairment would get out at the curb.

From the front, Baltimore Hebrew appears as accessible as St. Elizabeth since the synagogue does not have steps at its formal entrance. And like St. Elizabeth's parishioners, the Baltimore Hebrew congregants drive to services. Unlike St. Elizabeth, however, Baltimore Hebrew's secondary entrances—those closest to the parking lots—had steps. These secondary entrances have been ramped and a new accessible main entrance for both disabled and non-disabled has been built at the rear. This accessible door, which is at

FIGURE 18.3
Baltimore Hebrew, looking from the parking lot to the addition at the rear of the synagogue. Note the accessible walkway from parking to the building.

the back of an addition built behind the original synagogue building, faces an accessible walkway to the parking lot. Reserved parking spaces for people with mobility disabilities are closest to the building, but they still have to cross a driveway (Figure 18.3).

From the new entrance at the rear to the main sanctuary, two sets of steps blocked access. A large set of stairs, built in the addition, were ramped over (Figure 18.4). The smaller, second set at the back of the original building were replaced by a ramp. Now people in wheelchairs coming from parking spaces can enter either the side or rear entrance and have a level path to the sanctuary. But access in the sanctuary is very limited because the aisles are narrow and there are changes in level. The elevated pulpit area remains inaccessible. Baltimore Hebrew plans to make the sanctuary more accessible to people with mobility impairments. (The bathrooms already have been made more accessible.)

For people with hearing disabilities, Baltimore Hebrew has headsets in the sanctuaries to amplify sound, and it provides interpreters as needed for major holiday services. Also, the office has a text telephone. With an interpreter, Baltimore Hebrew's rabbi has taught courses on Judaism targeted for a deaf and hearing-impaired audience.

St. Elizabeth's aisles and narthex are wide and stepless, providing good accessible routes, and parishioners in wheelchairs have more than adequate room to sit in the aisles (Figure 18.5). The steps to the altar are not an obstacle since the priests bring commu-

FIGURE 18.4
Baltimore Hebrew, ramped stairs in addition.

FIGURE 18.5
St. Elizabeth, sanctuary.

nion to the congregants. The church has not added any assistive devices such as audio amplifications in the sanctuary or grab bars in the wide bathrooms because, according to Father Bloom, there has been no request for them.

The Americans with Disabilities Act specifically exempts religious buildings from its requirements so accessibility efforts will depend entirely on local codes and the good intentions of the congregation. Congregations housed in buildings designed in historical revival styles, despite their intentions, will find it hard to provide the degree of equal, dignified access that St. Elizabeth and Baltimore Hebrew, both designed in a nonhistorical style, do. Washington, D.C.'s most architecturally ambitious gothic revival church with its stepped entrance, for example, only provides access for a person in a wheelchair through a side entrance. But even the absence of a revival style does not assure good access to the building; a major Washington synagogue, designed in a modernist style, has only one accessible entrance, and it is the one farthest from the parking lot. Also, the physical separation between the audience and the people conducting the service, created primarily by elevating the altar area, is basic to religious structures, and St. Elizabeth's solution of having the priest step down to the congregants for communion only works as long as the priest does not have a mobility impairment. More than other public accommodations, religious buildings will probably provide limited accessibility and be slow to modify preferred architectural styles to provide better accessible designs; religious buildings have less legal incentive to be accessible, and traditional religious architectural expressions, both on the exterior and in the interior, inhibit full accessibility.

Chapter 19

CHINN AQUATICS & FITNESS CENTER

The 40-meter pool and the leisure/therapy pool, as well as the weight rooms and racquetball courts, are fully accessible at the Chinn Aquatics & Fitness Center, Prince William County, Virginia. In fact, the building, which opened in April 1991, and its parking lot are entirely accessible and, in addition, the center offers integrated and adapted exercise classes for customers with disabilities. This high degree of architectural and programmatic accessibility grew out of the close collaboration among the Prince William Park Authority as client, Sasaki Associates as landscape and building architect, and county residents as users (both people with disabilities and people without disabilities). Sasaki principal, Alan Resnick, AIA, wrote in *Parks & Recreation* (July 1992),

> What made the design review process particularly successful was the close involvement of the county staff who ultimately manage each space and direct its activities. . . . A particularly valuable member of the county's team was the special populations coordinator, who reviewed the designs for the entire facility to insure that it was appropriately accessible to the physically challenged of all ages.

Actually, the Park Authority's accessibility expert, Pam Sneed, CTRS, had two groups of people with disabilities or expertise in the field review the architect's plan.

Adjacent to the $10.4 million fitness center is Prince William County's Chinn Park Regional Library and Administrative Support Center, also designed by Sasaki Associates (Figure 19.1). Situated on a 77-acre county park, both buildings are two stories tall, but sited to appear as one-story buildings from the park entrance and parking lots (Figure 19.2). In front of and closest to each building is a row of accessible reserved parking, with curbcuts and posted signs. People with mobility impairments do not risk crossing traffic in the parking lot to get to the building (Figure 19.3). The entrance to the fitness center has manual doors and automatic doors that

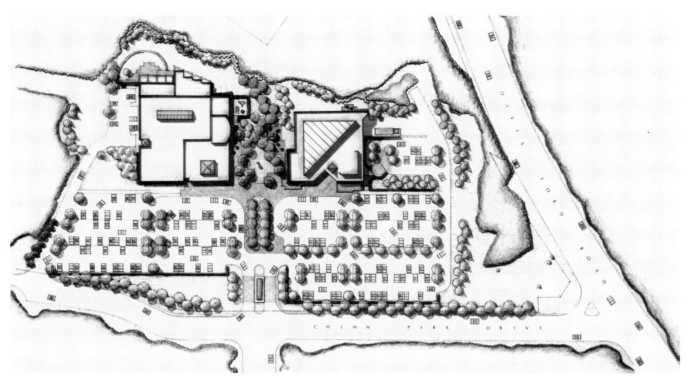

FIGURE 19.1
*Site plan of Chinn Regional Park. (From
Sasaki Associates. Reproduced by permission
of Sasaki Associates.)*

FIGURE 19.2
Chinn Aquatics & Fitness Center.

FIGURE 19.3
Reserved accessible parking next to Chinn
Aquatics & Fitness Center.

FIGURE 19.4
Entrance to Chinn Aquatics & Fitness
Center. Circular panel which opens right set
of doors is on the wall to the right of the
doors.

open when the wall panel is pressed (Figure 19.4). The entrance to
the library requires less effort; its automatic sliding doors are activated by a motion sensor. Each building has a secondary parking
lot with curbcuts but no reserved parking, and an entrance on the
lower level of the building. If the elevator in the fitness center were
out of order, people with mobility disabilities would enter the
building from the lower level and be on the same floor as the pools,

locker rooms, weight room and racquetball courts. In the library building, the upper floor is the regional library and the lower floor houses the county library system's administrative offices. Someone with a mobility impairment going to the administrative offices either parks in front and takes the elevator to the lower floor or parks on the side and enters the building on the administrative level. An elevator in two-story buildings exceeds code requirements and reflects the Park Authority's and the library's commitment to accessibility.

Resnick designed both buildings so that the spatial organization is straightforward and apparent to the visitor once inside the building's main entrance (Figures 19.5–19.7). On entering the library one sees the information desk with its large "information center" sign and beyond it the book stacks (Figure 19.8). To the right and rear of the information desk is the check-out desk. Both

LEGEND:

1. Men's Lockers
2. Women's Lockers
3. Weight/Exercize Room
4. Racquetball Court
5. Gymnasium
6. Sports Equipment
7. First Aid
8. Storage
9. Office
10. Natatorium
11. Leisure Pool
12. Whirl Pool
13. Filter Room
14. Mechanical Room
15. Electrical Room
16. Youth Lounge
17. Kitchen
18. Vending
19. Multipurpose Room
20. Lobby
21. Telephone
22. Racquetball Below
23. Gymnasium Below
24. Natatorium Below
25. Leisure Pool
26. Shower/Toilet
27. Play School Room
28. Young Child Nurser
29. Nursery
30. Sauna

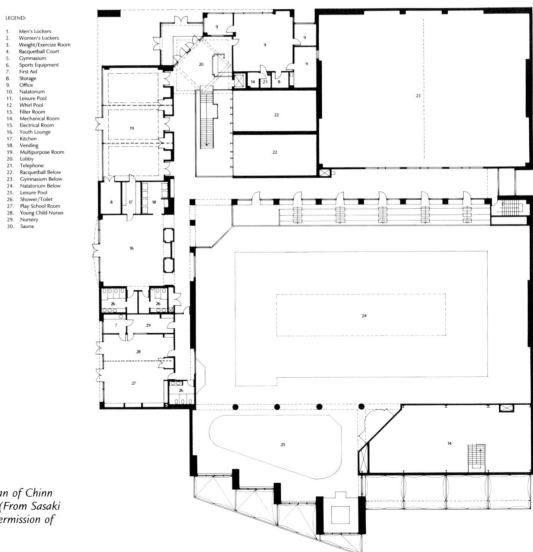

FIGURE 19.5
Second floor (main floor) plan of Chinn Aquatics & Fitness Center. (From Sasaki Associates. Reproduced by permission of Sasaki Associates.)

desks have lowered counter sections for people in wheelchairs or who are short. Also the desks with computer terminals are high enough for someone in a wheelchair to roll into the knee space. At the aquatics center, the two reception desks have counters with lowered sections. (Only the one desk designed by the architect is indicated on the plan.) At the stairs landing the carpeting ends, and the landing and threads have a hard rubber surface with bumps. The change in surface provides a tactile warning to someone who is visually impaired or blind, and the thread surface is also slip resistant. The organization of the second floors of the aquatics center and the library along a diagonal line invites visitors in, lessens confusion about where to go, and might make the facilities more manageable for people with developmental disabilities.

At the far end of the upper floor of the aquatics center are the viewing stands for the 40-meter pool. One section is stepped with

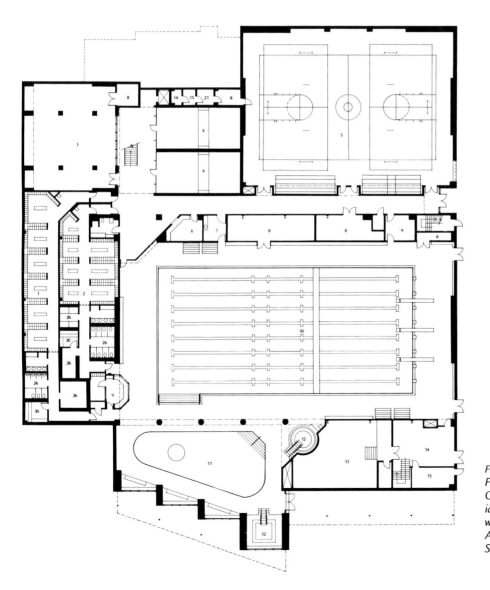

LEGEND:

1. Men's Lockers
2. Women's Lockers
3. Weight/Exercize Room
4. Racquetball Court
5. Gymnasium
6. Sports Equipment
7. First Aid
8. Storage
9. Office
10. Natatorium
11. Leisure Pool
12. Whirl Pool
13. Filter Room
14. Mechanical Room
15. Electrical Room
16. Youth Lounge
17. Kitchen
18. Vending
19. Multipurpose Room
20. Lobby
21. Telephone
22. Racquetball Below
23. Gymnasium Below
24. Natatorium Below
25. Leisure Pool
26. Shower/Toilet
27. Play School Room
28. Young Child Nursery
29. Nursery
30. Sauna

FIGURE 19.6
First floor plan of Chinn Aquatics & Fitness Center. The unisex bathroom, which is not identified on the plan, is adjacent to the women's locker entrance. (From Sasaki Associates. Reproduced by permission of Sasaki Associates.)

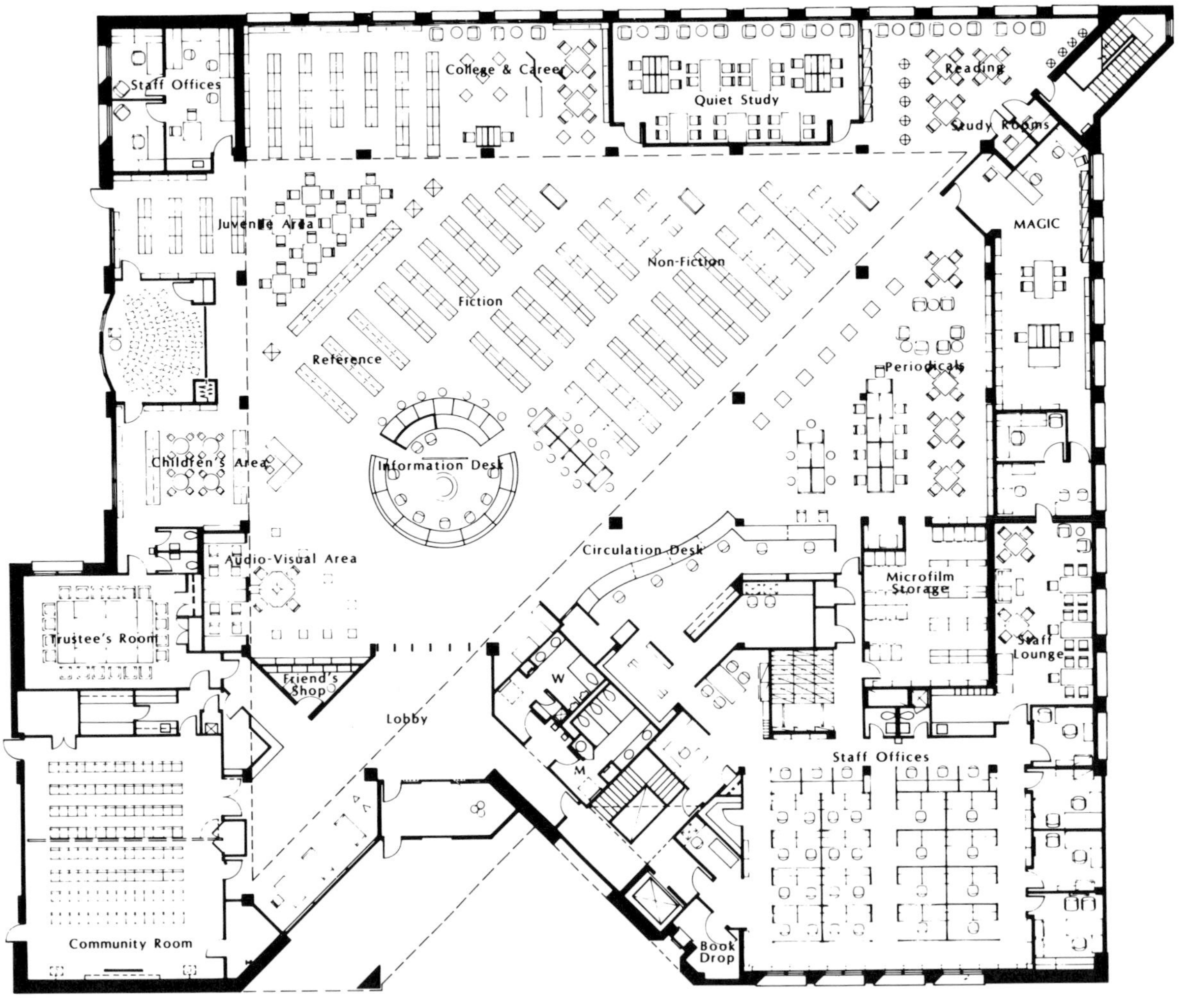

The floor plan shows the following labeled areas: Staff Offices, College & Career, Quiet Study, Reading, Study Rooms, Juvenile Area, Non-Fiction, MAGIC, Fiction, Reference, Periodicals, Children's Area, Information Desk, Audio-Visual Area, Circulation Desk, Microfilm Storage, Staff Lounge, Trustee's Room, Friend's Shop, W, M, Staff Offices, Lobby, Community Room, Book Drop

FIGURE 19.7
Second floor plan of Chinn Park Regional Library & Administrative Support Center. The second floor is the library; administration is on the first floor. (From Sasaki Associates. Reproduced by permission of Sasaki Associates.)

FIGURE 19.8
Chinn Park Regional Library. Information desk with lowered counter is on the left.

FIGURE 19.9
Chinn Aquatics & Fitness Center. Hydraulic seat lift in the foreground. In the background are the viewing stands. The elevated section with continuous railing on the left is for people in wheelchairs.

built-in benches and is inaccessible. Adjacent to it is a level surface viewing area intended for people in wheelchairs (Figure 19.9).

The corridor to the viewing stands has stationary exercise equipment along the walls. But the actual weight room is on the lower level, opposite the two racquetball courts. The entrances into these rooms, like all others in the center have no or low thresholds and are wide. Inside the weight room, all equipment is accessible; there are no steps or changes in level in the room. (Some private health clubs place free weights on stepped platforms, making them inaccessible for people with mobility disabilities who could other-wise lift weights.)

Down the first floor corridor from the weight room are the locker rooms, a unisex bathroom, and the pools. In addition to accessible sink, shower stall, and toilet, the locker rooms' other accessible features are high and low lockers, high and low mirrors, high and low hair dryers.

The unisex bathroom, adjacent to the locker rooms, is a convenience for a parent tending a child of the opposite sex and a necessity for the teenager or adult with an attendant of the other gender. This bathroom offers a much greater wheelchair turning area and a less sloped (for drainage) floor than the locker room, so it is also

FIGURE 19.10
Unisex bathroom, Chinn Aquatics & Fitness Center. The sink is high, has padded pipes and lever handles. The mirror is angled so that someone in a wheelchair can look up and see him or herself. The toilet is high, the toilet paper dispenser low, and there are two long grab bars. An emergency call button is located above the side grab bar, but there is no sign indicating its function.

FIGURE 19.11
Unisex bathroom, Chinn Aquatics & Fitness Center, showing lockers at different heights and changing bench along wall.

used by some people in wheelchairs who do not have or need attendants (Figures 19.10–19.12).

Although the 40-meter pool, the leisure/therapy pool, and whirlpool have steps, they are accessible, to varying degrees. Someone unable to descend the steps into the whirlpool can sit at the edge and swing his or her legs into the water. The 40-meter pool has a hydraulic chair lift, similar to the one at the National Rehabilitation Hospital (see Chapter 10), to lower someone into the

FIGURE 19.12
Unisex bathroom, Chinn Aquatics & Fitness Center, showing shower stall with adjustable, handheld shower head.

pool. The chair's occupant can regulate its movement as the control is mounted near the chair on the column; the lift at the rehabilitation hospital, however, is operated by an attendant outside the pool (Figure 19.9). At least one user of the 40-meter pool bypasses the stairs and the chair lift. He wheels to the edge of the pool, hops on his strong leg from the wheelchair into the water and then swims laps. The adjacent leisure/therapy pool has a "zero gravity" or "zero beach" end where there is no curb and the floor of the pool very gradually deepens (Figure 19.13). People roll into the leisure/therapy pool using the water wheelchairs supplied by the Chinn Center. By contrast, a public aquatic center in Rockville, Maryland, has handrails at the zero gravity end of its therapy pool to assist people walking into the pool; but it does not offer wheelchairs for use in the pool (Figure 19.14). The Rockville facility also does not have a chair lift for its lap pool; the lift was removed because it did not always clear the pool's edge, a problem Chinn does not have.

Lifting weights, swimming or exercising in the pools are activities in which one proceeds at one's own pace. For group activities, the Chinn Center offers "adapted" classes (e.g., in karate) for someone whose developmental or physical disability limits participation in programs for nondisabled people. The integration of the nondisabled and people with disabilities is the goal of the center, but it

FIGURE 19.13
Chinn Aquatics & Fitness Center,
leisure/therapy pool. Water wheelchair is
positioned at the "zero beach" end of the
pool.

believes there are circumstances where separate activities better serve its customers' needs.

Prince William County Park Authority augments its physical and programmatic accessibility by giving "barrier awareness training" to its employees. The course and accompanying manual describe various types of disabilities, the needs of people with those disabilities, and how to communicate effectively and interact with people who have disabilities.

Behind the reception desk at the Chinn Center is a large poster announcing the Authority's intent to comply with the Americans with Disabilities Act and encouraging people to contact the Authority's ADA committee. Forms for suggesting accessibility improvements or for pointing out inaccessible features are next to the poster. The Authority requires itself to investigate and respond to

FIGURE 19.14
*Montgomery County Department of
Recreation aquatic center, Rockville, MD,
showing the railings at the "zero beach" end
of the facility's leisure/therapy pool.*

all accessibility complaint forms within 10 days of the postmark. To ensure full consideration of any complaint, the facility manager must prepare a detailed response form and the Park Authority's ADA chairperson has to sign off on both the complaint and the response. In addition, all the Authority's facilities have been surveyed for accessibility, resulting in its "Americans with Disabilities Act Transitional Plan," dated June 24, 1992, which identifies needed changes and sets a timetable for the improvements at all sites. Two recommendations for the Chinn Center were to add signage and improve the unisex rest room by installing more grab bars, relocating the light switch, reducing the door weight, and widening the shower stall. The improved unisex shower stall will be probably be similar to the one in the Rockville Aquatic Center (Figure 19.15).

FIGURE 19.15
Montgomery County Department of Recreation aquatic center, Rockville, MD. Shower stall in unisex bathroom. The bench can be pivoted against the wall so that someone can shower while seated in a wheelchair.

The involvement of people with disabilities and disability experts in the design phase assured that the Chinn Aquatics & Fitness Center would be accessible; their continued involvement assures the oversights are corrected and the facility will become more accessible to the community, disabled and nondisabled. But no matter how good the designer and the accessibility consultants, it is the Park Authority's commitment to providing much more than code-required accessibility that is critical.

Chapter 20

WATERFRONT PARK

Charleston's new Waterfront Park is an extension of and a diversion from the city's historic downtown. Situated immediately east of the downtown, at the end of Vendue Range and running south to where it intersects Exchange Street, the park was built on an unused, debris-filled site, once part of Charleston's busy antebellum harbor. The park's grid layout and architectural details echo the street plan and houses of colonial Charleston (Figure 20.1). By drawing tourists to the water, the park is supposed to relieve crowding in the commercial and residential areas. At the same time, an additional tourist attraction has been created, and tourists and residents can now fish or stroll along the shore of the Cooper River. Waterfront Park succeeds admirably as subtly accessible urban design. It recaptures under-utilized space, preserves the natural environment, aids Charleston's commerce, and creates a setting where people regardless of race and wealth can mix.

Costing approximately $13.5 million, Waterfront Park was designed by Sasaki Associates, Inc., Watertown, MA, with Edward Pinckney Associates, Hilton Head, SC, landscape architect consultant, and Jacquelin T. Robertson, New York, NY, urban design consultant. Sakasi Associates (Stuart Dawson, FASLA, design principal) was required by the United States Army Corps of Engineers and the South Carolina Coastal Council to construct the park 3 to 4 feet above the high tide level and to leave undisturbed the marsh grasses along the water's edge. The logic of elevating the park was demonstrated when Hurricane Hugo struck Charleston in September 1989 and caused $1 million damage to trees, electrical/mechanical systems, and landscaping, but left intact the nearly completed park's structure.

In the early 1970s, a high-rise was proposed for the site and after that concept was scrapped, it took nearly 14 years to acquire the land, design, and build Waterfront Park. The park, which opened in May 1990, predates the Americans with Disabilities Act,

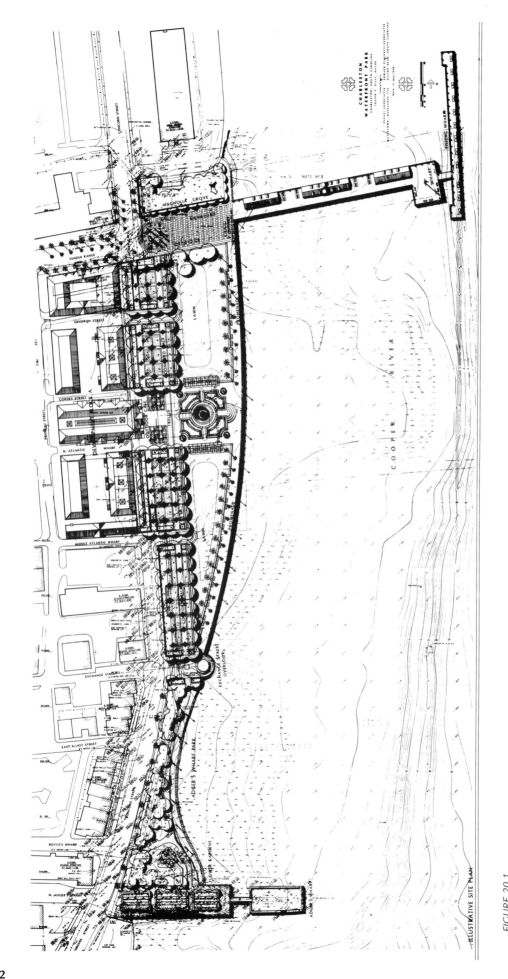

FIGURE 20.1
Site plan of Charleston Waterfront Park.
Development Block A, outdoor café, and
trellis are not yet built. (From Sasaki
Associates. Reproduced by permission of
Sasaki Associates.)

FIGURE 20.2
Looking across the parking lot to Waterfront Park with Pineapple Fountain to the right and wharf structure visible to the left.

but it reflects the designer's long corporate and personal history of addressing accessibility issues. In the 1960s, Stuart Dawson and Hideo Sasaki, the founder of Sasaki Associates, advised the University of Illinois at Urbana on making its buildings accessible. The firm believes it was one of the first to design a relief map (about 25 years ago, for Monument Square, Portland, ME). Mr. Dawson's sensitivity was further heightened when he had to use a wheelchair after knee surgery and again after a bike accident.

The accessibility issues at the Charleston Waterfront Park are (1) access to the park, which is elevated above the adjoining streets and parking lots, (2) accessible paths within the park, (3) access to decorative features, and (4) tactile maps (Figure 20.2). The current major entrance to the park is by steps up to the Vendue Fountain and the plaza and two wharves beyond it (Figures 20.3 and 20.4). At right angle to the Vendue Fountain stairs is North Gate, the ramped entrance to the more formal side of Waterfront Park (Figures 20.5 and 20.6). A second ramped entrance is at the south end of the park. According to Mr. Dawson, "In Charleston, which was designed following my first experience in a wheelchair, the ramps start at or close to the entry points to the park and end up in one of the most pleasant places in the park. Each [is] done with dignity and, in fact, gates which celebrate both ramps were designed by a local iron master in the best tradition of his craft."

Under the ADA accessibility guidelines, these ramps (7.5% incline) require handrails. In general, Sasaki Associates prefers lessening the incline of ramps to less than 1 : 20 so that they are no longer considered ramps under ADA guidelines and thus do not need handrails.

FIGURE 20.3
Looking from the plaza back toward Vendue
Fountain. Buildings behind the fountain are
on Vendue Range.

FIGURE 20.4
Four plaques tracing the growth of
Charleston. Beyond them are the wharf
structures.

FIGURE 20.5
North Gate, the ramped entrance at 90
degrees to the stairs at Vendue Fountain.

FIGURE 20.6
Looking from plaza in front of Pineapple
Fountain toward the back side of North
Gate.

Midway between these ramped entrances is Pineapple Fountain, the most ambitious and decorative feature of the park. The fountain is approached from the west by a very slight incline (Figure 20.7). Once buildings are erected on the parking lots adjacent to the park, this approach to the park and fountain will probably become the most popular entrance (Figures 20.1 and 20.2). The pineapple fountain is flanked by raised lawns and beyond is the promenade along the waterfront, leading to the wharves (Figure 20.8). The promenade is surfaced in gravel; the other paths in the park are brick, stone, or a combination of brick, gravel, and stone. Dawson's decision to use gravel was risky, but carefully thought out:

> In the middle 1970s we designed Boston Waterfront Park, and in the early 80s we designed the Enid Haupt Garden at the Smithsonian, prior to designing Charleston Waterfront Park in the late 80s and early 90s. A common denominator in all of the parks was accessibility.
>
> While gravel was used in each park, there is always another route—in each case, brick—from destination to destination. Perhaps the biggest disappointment with the exception of Boston Waterfront Park, is gravel as a material.
>
> At Boston the stone dust seems to work very nicely, compressing almost to the hardness of asphalt, but it sustains a gentleness that gravel brings to the quality of an urban park. . . . At the Smithsonian, the red gravel initially selected as a fitting setting to the Victorian, Eastern and Islamic Gardens was a disappointment. Initial complaints indicated that the gravel was tough for pushing strollers, although we observed several,

FIGURE 20.7
Low-incline approach to the Pineapple Fountain. Gravel waterfront promenade is beyond the fountain.

FIGURE 20.8
Looking from Pineapple Fountain to flanking lawn and beyond it to the promenade. The wharf is in the distance.

and was very dusty when dry and very muddy when wet. It was only later that we heard people with disabilities were having more trouble with it than originally thought. That gravel is now brick.

At Charleston Waterfront Park, a very complicated mixture of various gravels, clay and sand was selected. The intent was to produce a surface which would consolidate and harden over time. This seems to be happening in a majority of the gravel area, although some areas remain more granular, loose, and probably difficult to negotiate. Thus, the surface is definitely an issue, particularly gravel, although I would hope the Smithsonian is the only repaving that we will need to undertake, and that Charleston will compact over time much like Boston. Gravel is one of those wonderful materials that is not expensive and adds a humane touch to any public environment.

The Vendue and Pineapple Fountains, intended as decorative foci, have become more of a water playground for children than the designer ever anticipated. In light of that use, Dawson questions whether the pineapple fountain and its flanking lawns, which are used as playing fields, should be more accessible. (He views the Vendue Fountain as being accessible.) Even if the fountains were not used by children for water play, it would be appropriate for them to be accessible so that a person in a wheelchair who is visually disabled could feel the sculptured fountains.

The only features designed with the visually impaired in mind are the metal plaques near the wharf. With raised type and topographical lines and braille, the plaques trace four centuries of Charleston's growth (Figures 20.9 and 20.10).

In October 1992, three members of the Charleston mayor's Committee on Disabilities who use wheelchairs surveyed Waterfront Park for compliance with the ADA guidelines. They noted the

FIGURE 20.9
View of plaques with wharf in the background.

FIGURE 20.10
Close-up of the plaque showing nineteenth-century Charleston: raised typeface in lower left, braille in lower right, and raised map at top.

lack of handrails on the ramps, the lack of beveled nosing on the stairs, and they had trouble rolling on the gravel in less traveled parts of the paths. They did not echo Dawson's belief that the pineapple fountain and lawns should be more accessible. Neither Dawson's nor the surveyors' accessibility concerns have been raised by visitors in the two and a half years the park has been opened; only time will tell if all the gravel will compact and if the accessibility experts' concerns (and the ADA accessibility guidelines) were exaggerated.

Waterfront Park strikes one immediately with its beauty and diversity (of design motifs, users, and activities). Its accessible features are, by intention, less obvious. Stuart Dawson observed,

> Our goal was to provide handsome ramped access at each of the primary gateways into the park and to make each ramp as pleasant an experience as the steps leading more directly into the park. Interestingly, I've watched many people use the ramps instead of the stairs even though they don't need them. I suppose that is the ultimate test of a good resolution of access for people with disabilities, which is that people are just as inclined to use a ramp as they are to use adjacent steps. That should be all of our goals.

At Waterfront Park, the ramp has been elevated from an accessibility feature to a prominent design element.

Chapter 21

MOUNTAIN LAUREL TRAIL

Behind the National Wildlife Federation's Laurel Ridge Conservation Education Center in Vienna, Virginia, a series of a nature trails offer respite from the urban cacophony of nearby Washington, D.C. and show how nature provides animals with food, water, shelter, and a place to raise their young. One of the trails, the Mountain Laurel Trail, is a multisensory accessible trail 1.5 miles long running through 12 acres of woodlands (Figure 21.1). Dedicated in August 1986, the trail was intended as and has become a national model for accessible nature trails. The National Park Service recognized the importance of the Mountain Laurel Trail by designating it a National Recreation Trail.

The purpose of the National Wildlife Federation is to educate the public to appreciate the importance of natural conservation, which it does through publications, a summer camp, exhibitions, and demonstrations at its Laurel Ridge Center. With more than 5 million members and supporters, it is said to be the largest nonprofit conservation education organization in the United States.

Critical to the success of the accessible trail was the Federation's design process. First, a group of people with disabilities, disability experts, and organizations with expertise in the field were assembled to consult with the National Wildlife Federation (NWF) and its landscape architect, Guy Rando. More than 100 outdoor facilities across the country that considered themselves accessible were then surveyed by mail to ascertain which accessible features worked and which did not. Finally, the NWF's accessibility task force visited some local facilities that had made early efforts at accessibility. Thus, the final design draws on considerable personal experience, professional knowledge, and a very large sampling of earlier efforts.

The Mountain Laurel Trail is surfaced in smooth asphalt and is 5 feet wide, sufficient for a person in a wheelchair to turn around and for two people in wheelchairs to pass each other. The trail,

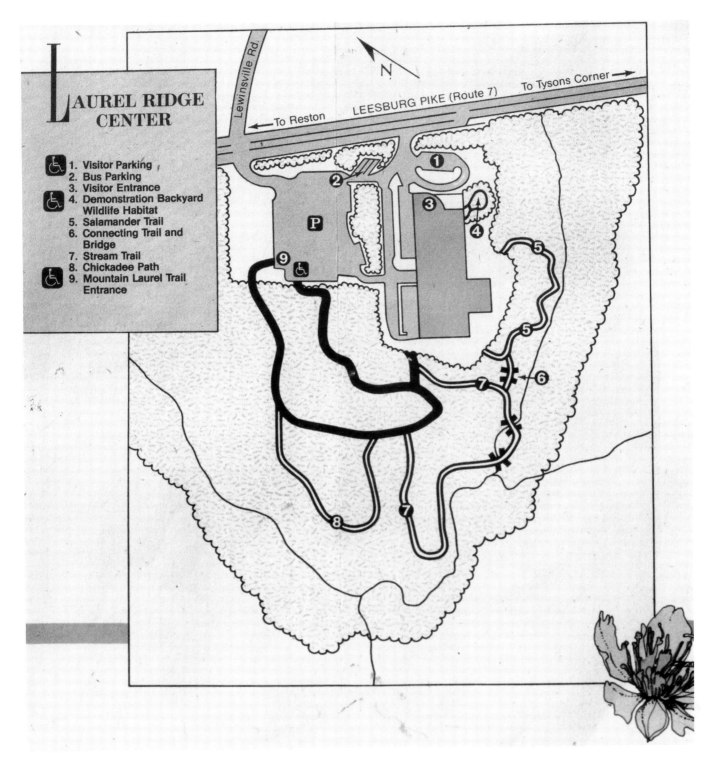

LAUREL RIDGE CENTER

1. Visitor Parking
2. Bus Parking
3. Visitor Entrance
4. Demonstration Backyard Wildlife Habitat
5. Salamander Trail
6. Connecting Trail and Bridge
7. Stream Trail
8. Chickadee Path
9. Mountain Laurel Trail Entrance

To Reston ← LEESBURG PIKE (Route 7) → To Tysons Corner

Lewinsville Rd.

FIGURE 21.1
Site plan of Laurel Ridge Conservation Education Center (Reproduced with permission of the National Wildlife Federation.)

which has ten interpretive stops and four rest areas, is essentially level, with very gradual turns, rises, and falls.

The entrance to the trail is from the parking lot, which has reserved parking for people with disabilities immediately adjacent to the pavilion entrance. Within the pavilion, a high-contrast (black lettering on white background) sign explains the features of the trail. All large interpretive signs along the trail are high contrast to be more legible to people with limited vision. Smaller signs identifying plants are also high contrast and have bright white rectangles mounted below them to attract the visitor's eye to the sign, which otherwise blends into the forest background. Large interpretive signs are angled and at a low height so they can be read by people in wheelchairs as well as those who stand. In front of and behind the pavilion, as well as at the other interpretive stops, two strips of gravel imbedded in epoxy provide a tactile and visual signal (the light color of the strip contrasts with the dark asphalt of the trail) so that the visitor is aware of entering an interpretive section on the trail (Figures 21.2 and 21.3). The signal tells a visually disabled person that it is time to refer to his or her large-print brochure, braille transcription of the signs, or to turn on the audio cassette player, all supplied by the NWF. While double strips indicate an interpretive stop, a single, raised gravel strip indicates a rest area (Figure 21.4). Benches at rest areas or interpretive stops are placed off to the side so as not to be a tripping obstacle to a visually impaired or blind visitor (Figure 21.5). Further reflecting the NWF's attention to the trailgoer's real needs, the benches are substantial rather than ornamental, with backs and armrests to provide adequate support. Wherever fences are needed along the trail for safety, they are low enough not to block the view of someone in a wheelchair.

FIGURE 21.2
Parking lot, reserved parking, and entrance pavilion to the accessible trail. Double strip of gravel indicates interpretive stop.

FIGURE 21.3
Sign in entrance pavilion. First set of double gravel strips indicates the end of the first interpretative stop. In background is the second set of strips indicating the second interpretive stop.

FIGURE 21.4
Rest stops are demarcated by single gravel strips. Sturdy benches are set back from the path. The low fence does not obstruct the view of someone in a wheelchair.

FIGURE 21.5
A large interpretive stop with double gravel strip. Bench is placed to avoid being a hazard to a visually impaired or blind visitor. Sign is angled and fence is low for people in wheelchairs.

Two trails without asphalt surfaces descend from the Mountain Laurel Trail, allowing some people with disabilities (or nondisabled persons) to get farther into the woodlands. High-contrast signs warn a visitor that he or she is leaving the wheelchair-accessible trail for a trail that is less accessible (or unaccessible for some people). The visitor may decide if he or she wants to try the trail.

The outgrowth of a deliberate and inclusive design process, the Mountain Laurel accessible trail enables people to explore the woodland independently and at their own pace, unencumbered (or at least less encumbered) by mobility or communication barriers.

The National Wildlife Federation views the accessible trail as being dynamic, always capable of improvement. Part of the effort to improve the trail includes its eventual expansion, using several surfacing materials other than asphalt so that their suitability and durability can be compared. According to the NWF's Roy Geiger, Jr., "The completion of a trail is not the end of the project, it is merely the end of the first phase—the construction phase. The challenge of maintaining, evaluating and revising the trail and its interpretative elements has just begun. Trails must evolve and improve if the visitor is to get the best experience possible."

Chapter 22

BALTIMORE WASHINGTON INTERNATIONAL AIRPORT

The United States Department of Transportation's "New Horizons for the Air Traveler with a Disability" details the requirements the Air Carrier Act of 1986 and the ADA impose on airports and airlines to provide better accessibility. The regulations for the Air Carrier Act, which affect airplanes, went into effect in April 1990 and those for ADA, which affect airports, became effective in January 1992. The Department of Transportation booklet, dated December 1991, states that, "with few exceptions, these services should be available in all carrier terminals within the next few years. . . ." Even before the booklet was published, the Baltimore Washington International Airport (approximately 10 miles from Baltimore and 30 miles from Washington) had met most of the public accommodation requirements of the ADA and exceeded a few.

Bill Jackson, manager of the BWI from 1984 to 1990, is usually credited as the driving force behind making the airport a leader in accessibility. He dates his interest to a 1985 meeting held at the airport in which Department of Transportation representatives, Architectural and Transportation Barrier Compliance Board (Access Board) representatives, and representatives of disability advocacy organizations discussed strategies for making air travel more accessible, especially for people in wheelchairs and those with hearing disabilities. "I was so impressed with some of the people at the meeting, people who were relegated to chairs, who had so much guts to be at the meeting and to travel. I thought airports should be leaders in making travel easier and less embarrassing. I wanted my airport to set the pace and be the example that others might follow." Based on his observations of travelers with disabilities at BWI, the advice of the former directors of Maryland's Commission on People with Disabilities (both of whom use wheelchairs), and recommendations made by disability consultants such as Corporate Services for the Deaf, Jackson had several accessibility features at the airport installed during his tenure.

Since the early 1980s, travelers who were deaf or who had limited hearing had been complaining to the Access Board that they needed text telephones at airports so they could call airports from the outside and for them to use when they were in airports. To evaluate the usefulness of this request, the Access Board and the Department of Transportation arranged in the mid-1980s for BWI, a single-terminal facility, and Miami International Airport, a multi-terminal facility, to add portable text telephones. (Miami already had a single older model text telephone.) Baltimore placed one text telephone at the central information desk which is open during the day and early evening and the second one at the police office, which is always open. Subsequently, BWI has added another portable text telephone, installed a permanent pay text phone, and installed shelves and electrical outlets at some pay telephone banks for travelers using their own portable text telephones (Figure 22.1). The airport has also installed five monitors that provide visual display of public address audio announcements and run additional information (e.g., locations of text telephones) to help hearing-impaired and deaf travelers (Figure 22.2). The visual pagers are strategically placed throughout the terminal: near the information desks and entrances to the concourses on the second floor and at the international gate on the first floor of BWI's horseshoe-shaped terminal building (Figure 22.3).

The compact, single-terminal layout of BWI benefits non-disabled and disabled travelers alike by reducing the distance to gates and anxiety about missing flights; the parking arrangements also serve well the needs of both disabled and nondisabled travelers. The wide, clearly marked reserved parking for people with disabilities in the garage adjacent to the terminal are next to the elevators and the walkways, with curbcuts at both ends (Figure 22.4). At the

FIGURE 22.1
Row of pay telephones at Baltimore Washington Airport, with the last telephone having a text telephone unit. Note the two large signs indicating text telephone.

FIGURE 22.2
Visual pager centrally located at concourse
C near security check point, escalator, and
route to other concourses and to parking
garage.

FIGURE 22.3
Map showing accessible features. (From
BWI Special Services & Access Guide.
Reproduced by permission of the Maryland
Aviation Authority.)

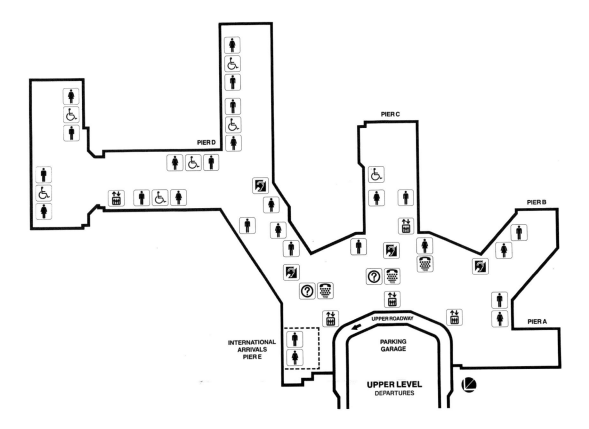

FIGURE 22.4
Walkway from terminal to parking garage, with elevator and reserved accessible parking just beyond the covered portion of the walkway.

long-term, less expensive satellite parking lots, the reserved parking spaces are next to the bus shelters. Free shuttle buses run between the lots and the terminals, and the wheelchair-accessible shuttle bus, also free, can be reserved in advance for service between the terminal, satellite parking and the BWI train station. People with disabilities can park for 15 minutes or less specially marked spaces right in front of the terminal.

Inside the terminal, several recent changes have improved accessibility for people in wheelchairs. An automatic teller machine, pay telephones, and water fountains have been lowered. The water fountains, with clear knee space to allow someone in a wheelchair to approach the fountain straight on as well as from the side, are recessed so as not to be a tripping hazard to a traveler with a visual disability. In the bathrooms, some counters, handles and urinals have been changed to be accessible and additional improvements are planned. At present, narrow stalls with parallel grabs are considered accessible. Those stalls will be widened and a rear grab bar added.

The most important accessibility accommodation for people in wheelchairs is the airport's five unisex bathrooms. Not only do they allow someone with an attendant or family member of the opposite gender to assist, each offers a wide wheelchair turning radius, cantilevered sinks with recessed pipes, lever handles, angled mirrors, and lowered soap dispensers (Figure 22.5). Also next to the toilet is an emergency button which lights a beacon outside the door, summoning airport personnel. The toilet not only has a permanent side grab bar next to the emergency button and the permanent rear grab bar, but also an adjustable side bar to the right of the toilet (Figures 22.6 and 22.7). The right side bar can be raised for people who

FIGURE 22.5
Unisex bathroom sink and other fixtures.

FIGURE 22.6
Unisex bathroom toilet with permanent and
adjustable grab bars. Note the emergency
button with instructions.

FIGURE 22.7
Unisex bathroom—the only one with
automatic door and lock. Emergency beacon
is above the door.

transfer to the toilet from a wheelchair and find the grab bar more hindrance than help. For others, either in wheelchairs or using walking aids, two close parallel bars are preferable and the right grab bar can be left down. (See Chapter 10 on the National Rehabilitation Hospital and Chapter 8 on Henry Viscardi High School for similar grab bar configurations.) People who use wheelchairs or other mobility aids have different types of mobility disabilities and need various and different supports in transferring to toilets. The grab bar arrangement at BWI's unisex bathroom provides the flexibility to meet many different needs.

When the text telephones were first installed at BWI, the signs indicating their existence and location were too small and unlikely to be seen. The other means used to inform the public of accessible services at BWI—press releases and brief descriptions in airport publications—also were of limited value. The airport management worked with its consultants, Corporate Services for the Deaf and Apple Design, to improve the signage and publications to better inform travelers of all accessible features of BWI. The newly published "BWI Special Services & Access Guide" provides precise information on accessible parking, unisex bathrooms, visual paging, text telephones, and other accessible features. Printed in large bold type, the brochure unfolds to an easily comprehensible map of the terminal showing the location of all accessible features (Figure 22.3). By contrast, the older wall maps at the airport have not yet been updated to show accessible features. Although its efforts are not complete, BWI appreciates the importance of informing people of accessible services, rather than relying on the people who need the services to inquire about their availability. At other public accommodations where volunteers or paid staff at information desks are expected to answer questions on available accessibility services, they often provide incomplete or wrong information.

The drive to make BWI accessible might have been provided by one individual, Bill Jackson, but the effort to refine accessibility at the airport is now driven by the Americans with Disabilities Act. To ensure compliance with the ADA accessibility guidelines, the airport management conducted a self-evaluation of accessibility early in 1992 and then asked representatives from disability organizations to tour the facility and critique it in terms of the ADA requirements. Many of the recommendations that grew out of the self-evaluation and tours by outside experts were incorporated in the "Maryland Aviation Administration Transition Plan for the Americans with Disabilities Act." The plan specifies how to improve accessibility and sets a timetable for making the recommended changes. Adopted on July 26, 1992, the second anniversary of the signing of the ADA, the plan includes sensitivity training, adding braille terminal maps and other tactile signage, removing inappropriate language and questions from personnel manuals and job applications, and removing remaining physical barriers at the terminal and related facilities. The Americans with Disabilities Act imposed on BWI a formal, institutionalized approach to achieving accessibility, which is more likely to have greater permanent benefits than the previous approach that depended on key personnel being committed to accessibility.

The Americans with Disabilities Act will also significantly broaden the range of accessibility services offered at BWI. The May 1985 meeting at the airport focused on the accessibility needs of those in wheelchairs or with hearing disabilities. The accessibility features installed between 1986 and 1991 at the airport addressed the needs of the mobility and hearing disabled. But in 1992, under the ADA-mandated review, a representative of the visually impaired and blind community toured the airport terminal, evaluated its accessibility features, and made recommendations pertaining to that group's specific accessibility needs. If his recommendations, covering ADA-required tactile signage, low-vision and nonvisual communication techniques, and his general statements on appropriate attitudes and behavior toward people with disabilities (see Section VI overview) are adopted by BWI, it will correct the major accessibility omission at the airport.

Chapter 23

HYATT REGENCY RESTON

In March 1991, Evan J. Kemp, Jr., chairman of the United States Equal Employment Opportunities Commission, traveled to Chicago to praise the Hyatt Hotels Corporation. He said, "Hyatt is stepping out in front and setting an example for American business. . . . When a company like Hyatt makes its business accessible, it opens the doors of its hotels to a whole new universe of customers and employees." Mr. Kemp was responding to Hyatt president Darryl Hartley-Leonard's announcement that his hotels would be "as barrier free as possible by the year 1995." Hyatt's newer hotels demonstrate that the chain is already a leader in hotel accessibility.

At the press conference, Hartley-Leonard unveiled a four-part accessibility program. Hyatt would recruit nationally to hire people with disabilities, have "focus groups of travelers with disabilities to determine firsthand their special service needs; [have] sensitivity training for Hyatt employees to make them more aware of the special service needs of hotel guests with disabilities. . . ." The fourth initiative is to develop guidelines for building barrier-free new hotels and renovating existing hotels to be as accessible as possible. Barrier Free Environments, Inc. of Raleigh, North Carolina is assisting with the guidelines.

One of the newer Hyatts is the architectural landmark of a new shopping complex in Reston, VA. Anchoring the most prominent side of the Reston Town Center, the Hyatt Regency Reston is the gateway to this upscale commercial center, which emulates the variety, vitality, and pedestrian orientation of a European town square. RTKL Associates of Washington, D.C. were project architects for the hotel, which opened in October 1990, and Wilson Associates of Dallas designed the interior.

The hotel's welcoming gateway starts with its curved driveway, which is level with the entrance, eliminating curb barriers. Paralleling the curve of the driveway is an arcade to the hotel parking garage, where "handicapped parking" is closest to the hotel. Wheth-

FIGURE 23.1
Hyatt Regency Reston driveway and
entrance.

er a guest (with a disability) gets out of the car at the hotel entrance or comes from the garage, the distance is short, and under cover. Bollards protect pedestrians from vehicular traffic (Figure 23.1).

Once inside the hotel, the reception desk is to the left, a two-story-high, skylit conservatory is straight ahead, and to the right an on-grade corridor leads to the restaurant and to the elevator lobby. The attractive restaurant has neither cumbersome thresholds nor level changes, which are common in many other restaurants. From the elevator lobby a ramp with handrails on both sides offers a second route to the conservatory. From the conservatory another wide corridor flanked by retail establishments and a restaurant goes to the pedestrian plaza in the Reston Town Center. The path for the person with a disability from the hotel lobby to either restaurant or elevator (which rings at each floor and has raised numbers, braille and illuminated buttons) is as direct, easy, and thought-out as the relationship among driveway, garage, and hotel entrance.

On the second floor, all of the banquet and meeting rooms, the telephone banks, water fountains, and bathrooms are accessible. The telephones, with amplified headsets, are mounted at the height and with knee space for someone in a wheelchair. The fountains are lowered, but are suspended in a wide alcove so that they do not pose a hazard for a visually impaired guest. In the bathroom, the first stall is wider and has grab bars and the first sink has recessed pipes and lever handles. Placing the wider stall at the front rather

FIGURE 23.2
Second floor bathroom.

than its usual location at the end of the bathroom is more convenient for someone with a mobility impairment, but only using levers at the first sink and designating that with a plaque as being for people with disabilities is insensitive (Figure 23.2).

Of the hotel's 514 guest rooms, 12 are designed for people with disabilities. The doors are wider and have a lower peephole and lever handles. There is maneuvering room in the corridor and in the room so that someone can open the door without extra repositioning of his or her wheelchair. The bathroom has grab bars at the toilet and in the shower stall and wheelchair clearance under the sink (Figure 23.3). The shower stall has a seat, adjustable handheld shower head, and a low lip on the edge of the stall, easing transfer from a wheelchair to the shower seat. The low lip also benefits anyone who has trouble raising his or her legs to step in or out of the shower. (The same type of shower stall is in the employees' locker room, see Figures 23.4 and 23.5.) The closet opposite the bathroom has a lowered clothes rack. The room offers good wheelchair clearance, and for the hearing impaired there is a visual as well as an audible fire alarm (Figure 23.6). The accessible guest rooms in this Hyatt and in other hotel chains should be closer to the elevators for the convenience of people with mobility impairments.

At the March 1991 press conference, Hartley-Leonard said "It is not that we've ignored the situation in the past. We've always followed the state and local building codes that define accessibility. It's just that we may not have done enough." The Hyatt Regency Reston accurately reflects Hartley-Leonard's perceptions. Features covered by code such as bathrooms, water fountains, and desig-

FIGURE 23.3
Guest room toilet and sink.

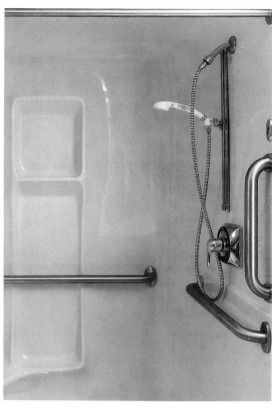

FIGURE 23.4
Guest room shower stall.

FIGURE 23.5
Employee shower stall. Soap dispenser
should be lower.

175

FIGURE 23.6
Guest room. Notice the visual fire alarm.

nated guest rooms are accessible. But where the architectural statement is made—at the front desk (too high for a person in a wheelchair or of short stature), at the front door (hinged doors and a revolving door rather than an electric sliding door), and at the conservatory (needlessly separated from the front lobby by steps)—accessibility is limited or absent. The March 1991 declaration means that Hyatts with good accessibility in part, like the Reston hotel, will become comprehensively accessible.

Chapter 24

CHEESECAKE FACTORY

The Cheesecake Factory is not an obvious example of an accessible public accommodation. The restaurant's most prominent features are, in fact, inaccessible—its high bar, stools and tables on the first floor, and the stairs from the first floor bar to the second floor restaurant. Even several of the accessible features of the second floor miss the ADA accessibility guidelines by a few inches. The restaurant opened in January 1991, 6 months after the ADA was signed into law, but 6 months before the guidelines were published in their final version in the *Federal Register;* therefore, the Cheesecake Factory was built to the pre-ADA accessibility codes. Most importantly, nevertheless, the restaurant demonstrates that the vendor's attitude is critical to providing public accessibility.

Designed by architect Russell J. Werth, the Cheesecake Factory anchors the corner of a new retail/office/hotel complex in upper northwest Washington, D.C. Of the mall's three pedestrian entrances, the most prominent one, located at the corner of the complex where two major streets intersect, is inaccessible because of stairs. The hotel's entrance is the most accessible, having automatic sliding doors. The third pedestrian entrance is adjacent to the Cheesecake Factory. A few feet from this entrance is the metro (subway) elevator. Someone in a wheelchair has good access to the stores, hotel, offices, or the restaurant by subway, the parking garage, and, to a lesser degree (at least symbolically if not physically), from the sidewalk.

There are four public entrances to the Cheesecake Factory. On the second floor, double doors lead from the mall to the restaurant. On the first floor, just inside the mall's doors, a single door opens to the Cheesecake Factory. On the other side of the mall's double doors, the restaurant has a revolving door and next to it a single door that provide access from the sidewalk. It is interesting that the less accessible first floor has two narrow doors and a revolving door, while the accessible second floor has wide double doors.

FIGURE 24.1
Second floor entrance to the Cheesecake Factory, looking from the restaurant toward the mall.

The first floor of the Cheesecake Factory is a small space, and the area near the bar seems crowded even when there are few patrons—hardly an inviting passageway for someone in a wheelchair. Along the window facing the street and along an adjacent wall, however, there are banquettes and the tables in front of them are wheelchair accessible. The bartenders and servers will serve the same drinks and light fare to someone in a wheelchair sitting in the accessible area as to someone sitting at the high bar or adjacent high tables and stools, but the inaccessible space is the focus of the design on the first floor of the Cheesecake Factory.

Someone in a wheelchair entering the first floor of the Cheesecake Factory and desiring a full course meal will be directed by the host to take the mall elevator to the second floor and proceed to the restaurant's entrance on that floor. If needed, the host will escort a patron to the elevator and then to the restaurant's upper-story entrance.

FIGURE 24.2
Women's bathroom with accessible stall.

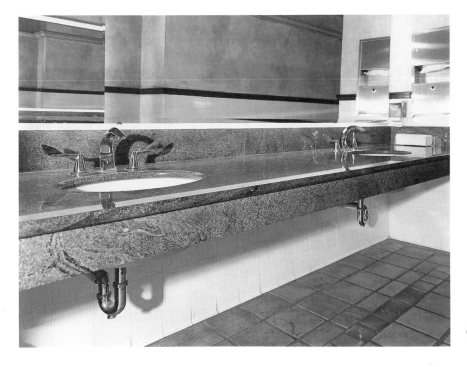

FIGURE 24.3
Women's bathroom with accessible sink.

In contrast to the tight feel of the bar area, the restaurant is quite open, with wide entrance and passageways. Just inside the restaurant's doors are lowered telephones and just beyond them, off a cross corridor, are the accessible bathrooms (Figure 24.1). The toilet stall in the women's room is wide and deep, with the requisite grab bars and lowered paper dispenser (Figure 24.2). The bathroom counter has open knee space running its entire length, the drain pipes are recessed (one more than the other), and paper towels are on the counter for women unable to reach the dispenser. Also, the sinks have lever handles rather than knobs, as the latter require more dexterity (Figure 24.3). The accessible bathrooms in most

FIGURE 24.4
Row of accessible tables where a chair would be removed to seat a patron in a wheelchair.

public accommodations have only one sink with padded (or recessed) pipes, knee space and lever handles, whereas the other sinks remain inaccessible, suggesting separate, but (supposedly) equal facilities. The Cheesecake Factory made all its sinks accessible.

Most new restaurants seem to have tables high enough to clear the armrests of wheelchairs, with bases small enough not to block wheelchair or the person using it, but often a person in a wheelchair is seated half in the aisle and half at the table. The Cheesecake Factory only designates as wheelchair accessible those tables on wide aisles (Figures 24.4 and 24.5). It does not suffice that the restaurant consider the table accessible. According to the restaurant's procedures manual, the host must specifically ask a person in a wheelchair if he or she is comfortable at that table.

For patrons with limited vision, the restaurant offers a large-print menu and a braille version for people who are blind. Knowing from experience that people with low vision prefer, at lunch, to sit

FIGURE 24.5
Accessible booth, where someone in a
wheelchair could sit comfortably at the end
of the table.

near the window, the host tries to accommodate that wish. The host and server are also reminded by the restaurant manual that people with mobility or other disabilities might take longer to get to the table, to order, and to eat, so the staff are required to be patient and to provide any extra help that might be desired. The manual also instructs the host to seat a party needing an accessible table as soon as one becomes available—ahead of other people waiting. And if a party with hearing-impaired people is waiting, the host is to ask where they will be and to offer to get them when their table is available.

Shortly after the Cheesecake Factory opened, a woman in a wheelchair wrote to the manager complaining of the inaccessibility of the restaurant's bar. The manager invited the woman to return and suggest improvements. She came back and brought along a friend who is a disability advocate. The Cheesecake Factory management listened to them and made at least some of the recommended changes. To be sensitive to the feelings and needs of people with disabilities is also emphasized in the restaurant's manual, which has a specific section entitled "Serving guests with disabilities."

> When dealing with someone who has a disability speak directly to the person rather than through a companion who may be along. Always assume that the person is capable of communicating and knows best how to convey their thoughts to others. . . . Not all hearing impaired persons can lip-read. Those who do will rely on facial expression and body language to help in understanding. Show consideration by placing yourself facing the light source and keeping your hands away from your mouth when speaking. Shouting won't help. Written notes will. *If you are offered a pad and pencil, use it* [emphasis added].*

Accessibility in public accommodations means more than eliminating physical barriers and improving communications; it means that everyone is treated courteously and efficiently—as demonstrated at the Cheesecake Factory, which is always crowded with nondisabled and disabled patrons.

---

*The Cheesecake Factory manual's section on disability was based on a National Easter Seal Society publication, *Awareness Is the First Step Towards Change: Tips for Disability Awareness*. With the exception of the last sentence the quote is from the Easter Seal publication, with a few words changed by The Cheesecake Factory. The last sentence was written by The Cheesecake Factory.

Section VII

OFFICES AND GOVERNMENT BUILDINGS

Since the founding of the country, when Jefferson convinced Washington that competitions should be held for the designs of the president's house and the Capitol building, the national government has appreciated the symbolic value of architecture. Exactly 200 years later, federal office buildings are becoming accessible, in symbolic expression of the government's commitment to the civil rights of people with disabilities. Some already accessible federal agencies have achieved better accessibility by moving to newer, plusher offices, designed around new modular furniture. Others are making substantial architectural changes to their older, historic buildings. For government offices as well as private offices, accessibility is created through a blending of architecture, interior design, and assistive technology.

At the Supreme Court and the Capitol, the temporary wooden ramps that provided the exterior accessible paths to the entrances have been replaced by permanent stone ramps that are more in keeping with the buildings' architecture. The physical, architectural changes made outside the buildings are augmented by physical and assistive technology changes made inside. More accessible bathrooms are planned, and floor annunciators are being installed in elevators. At the Justice Department's Great Hall, an unsatisfactory chair lift was replaced by two elegant ramps, a case where an architectural solution was preferred over an assistive-technology solution.

Other federal agencies—the Equal Employment Opportunity Commission (EEOC), The Access Board, and the President's Committee on Employment of People with Disabilities (PCEP)—moved to new buildings, which had few or no architectural barriers to overcome. Using adjustable modular furniture, the interior designers created work spaces where people in wheelchairs can maneuver, have enough knee clearance at their desks, and can reach their wall cabinets. Of course, the public spaces—corridors, bathrooms, kitchens, etc.—are also accessible for someone in a wheelchair. To a limited degree, these federal agencies employ assistive technology to improve accessibility. Doors can be opened by pushing a button. Scanners, video monitors, and computer software assist workers who are visually impaired or blind to read and prepare documents.

While symbolic of the federal government's commitment to people with disabilities, the offices also demonstrate that an accessible office looks no different than an inaccessible one. The accessible office is neither more nor less attractive, and its design was not obviously influenced by accessibility requirements. In fact, the highly accessible, newly renovated offices of the Paralyzed Veterans of America are more impressive and more dignified than the less accessible offices of other organizations.

When the National Organization on Disability moved, it selected a building near the White House, a location of great prestige and symbolic value for Washingtonians, and a building with wide, level plazas to the front door, offering good accessible paths for someone in a wheelchair. Unfortunately the elevator button for NOD's floor is too high for someone in a wheelchair. However, NOD added a lever to press the sixth floor button, demonstrating that low-level assistive technology is sometimes the only technology required.

The more common and more sophisticated assistive technology in the office is the computer. At the EEOC and the PCEP, computer software and hardware enlarges text on the screens and on documents, or reads aloud documents placed on scanners. In the opinion of the PCEP's computer expert, computers coupled with modems and special software, will supplant text telephones for people with hearing and/or speech disabilities. By modifying, replacing, or eliminating the traditional computer keyboard, people with limited or no muscular control can operate computers (Figure VII.1). A person can control a computer with a beam of light, flick of his or her eyelashes, voice commands, or by puffs of air from a straw in his or her mouth. Assistive technology, ranging from the simple elevator button lever or automatic door to sophisticated computers enables more people with disabilities to work and enables people with more extensive disabilities to work.

Assistive technology is also increasingly common in vehicles, ranging from hand controls for the gas and brake pedals to electric and electronic controls for nearly everything in the vehicle. Also, the ADA requires greater accessibility in public transportation systems. More people with disabilities, therefore, using their own cars, private vans, taxicabs, buses, or subways, are able to get to work.

People with disabilities need an accessible path from the vehicle to the office building and then to the office. Curbcuts, unobstructed sidewalks, easily opened doors, accessible parking garages, and accessible elevators are the critical elements along the path from transportation to the accessible office.

Accessible office design consists of three aspects. Phase one is removing the architectural barriers, whether they are, for example, the lack of curb cuts at the sidewalk in front of the building or the narrow doors with thresholds inside the building. Phase two is creat-

FIGURE VII.1
National Rehabilitation Hospital, REquest Rehabilitation Engineering Center. The position of a computer monitor, the type of keyboard, and even the means of controlling the computer can be changed to suit the needs of the operator. Such flexibility benefits the nondisabled as well as the operator with disabilities.

ing spaces and furnishings that are wide enough, clear enough, low enough, or high enough to be accessible to someone in a wheelchair. The third phase involves applying the appropriate assistive technology to help people perform functions that would otherwise be difficult or impossible because of their disabilities.

As assistive technology becomes more pervasive and basic to the workplace, the architect and interior designer will move beyond eliminating physical barriers to creating the physical environment most conducive for the use of assistive technology by workers with disabilities. For example, part of the top of the desk in Figure VII.1 is clear so that a monitor can be mounted below rather than above eye level. Furniture that permits flexibility in placing computer components is more ergometric, better suited to, and, therefore, more efficient for the particular needs of the office worker, with or without disabilities. Also, the assistive technology for the visually disabled and blind discussed in Chapter 9 has tremendous potential implications for building design and office planning.

Chapter 25

THE PARALYZED VETERANS OF AMERICA HEADQUARTERS

The Paralyzed Veterans of America (PVA), chartered by the United States Congress, is a non-profit organization dedicated to serving the needs of its members-all of whom have catastrophic paralysis caused by spinal cord injury or disease. [From PVA mission statement.]

With 15,000 members, a board, and several senior managers who use wheelchairs, the PVA's 10-year-old headquarters building—a mere three blocks from the White House—has always been accessible. But with its 1991–1992 renovation, the building's interiors have been upgraded and its accessibility refined.

The new spaces were designed by Kim Beasley, AIA, who directs the PVA's Architecture and Barrier Free Design program, and the Washington, D.C. office of RTKL. Through the Architecture and Barrier Free Design program, the PVA and Beasley have advised several institutions and corporations on improving accessibility. For the new Orioles Park at Camden Yards, Beasley was the only architect on the accessibility committee that developed the equal access chair for the stadium and Beasley/PVA has been awarded a patent for the chair design (see Chapter 17). Beasley and his associate at the PVA, Thomas Davies, AIA, have also coauthored two books on accessibility in hotels and in housing. Therefore, the renovation of the PVA building reflects not only RTKL's interior design expertise but also Beasley's several years of designing and advising on accessible design and his years of observing how his colleagues in wheelchairs use the building.

At the building's entrance, the door at the extreme right, closest to the guard's desk, can be opened automatically by the push plate, adjacent to the intercom, on the pier in front of the building (Figure 25.1). Like all the push plates in the building (e.g., at the bathrooms and at the guard desk), this plate is along the accessible path so the person using it does not have to detour to reach it or remaneuver his or her wheelchair after using it to get to the door.

FIGURE 25.1
Paralyzed Veterans of America building with automatic door to the right. Notice the push plate and telephone on the pier in front of building closest to door side.

FIGURE 25.2
Guard's desk with lowered counter in the Paralyzed Veterans of America building. Push plate to open the front door is mounted on the guard desk. Once someone in a wheelchair presses the plate, he or she wheels straight out the slow-moving door without having to reposition the wheelchair.

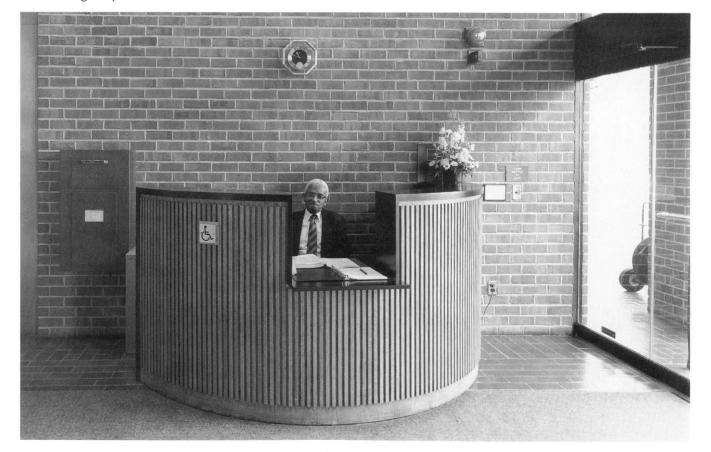

Also, all the automatic doors open and close slowly allowing plenty of time for a person in a wheelchair or using walking aids to get through. Just inside the front doors, the guard's desk has a lowered counter at the right height for people in wheelchairs (Figure 25.2).

Although the first floor elevator lobby is unchanged, those on the upper floors have been redesigned. They have been enlarged, providing more room for maneuvering a wheelchair and making the paths between elevator and offices more direct. Also, the lobbies have cantilevered shelves that, besides supporting flower vases, could be used by someone in a wheelchair waiting for an elevator to write a note, rest a package, or sort papers (Figure 25.3).

Before the renovation, the tenth floor elevator lobby had a reception desk facing the elevators. The windows behind the receptionist created glare that made it uncomfortable for visitors to address the receptionist. (It would have been especially troublesome for a visitor who was hearing impaired and more dependent on seeing the receptionist clearly, see Figure 25.4.) The desk has been moved away from the windows to in front of the new wall separating the board room from the reception lobby (Figures 25.5 and 25.6). The renovated wall opposite the receptionist has a couch and table flanked by new wood panels. Also, the acoustical ceiling has been replaced with a more architectonic treatment (Figure 25.7). The renovated reception lobby seems larger and is made more elegant and unified by the use of wood.

FIGURE 25.3
Elevator lobby on an upper floor, providing generous space for maneuvering a wheelchair and providing direct paths to the offices.

FIGURE 25.4
Prerenovation tenth floor reception desk with glare created by backlighting from the windows.

FIGURE 25.5
Prerenovation tenth floor reception lobby, with the board room on the other side of the wall.

FIGURE 25.6
Tenth floor reception desk after renovation. Besides being more elegant, the new reception desk is out of the glare.

FIGURE 25.7
Renovated tenth floor reception lobby with new reception desk, new wall separating the board room from the lobby, and new seating area. Doors from the board room to the corridor (not visible) have also been redesigned and made more attractive.

A similar wood treatment is repeated in the adjacent board room where screens, easels, and other audiovisual equipment and supplies are stored behind wooden cabinets when not in use. Like all cabinets and nonautomatic doors in the building, minimal strength and dexterity are needed to open them. Beyond the board room, the executive committee workroom provides board members with telephones, computers, and work surfaces at desks accessible for someone in a wheelchair (Figure 25.8).

Around the corner from the board room is one of the PVA's two fully accessible kitchenettes. Even the counter for the coffee maker was designed low so that the machine would be at the right height for someone in a wheelchair. Knee space under the counter next to the sink enables a person in a wheelchair to make his or her own snack. Where there is not knee space for a straight on approach, someone in a wheelchair can still reach the kitchen appliances such as the microwave by reaching out to the side (Figure 25.9). The cabinets are not only within reach of someone in a wheelchair, but they require only slight pressure or pull to open or close them.

FIGURE 25.8
Renovated executive committee work room with accessible work stations is next to the board room.

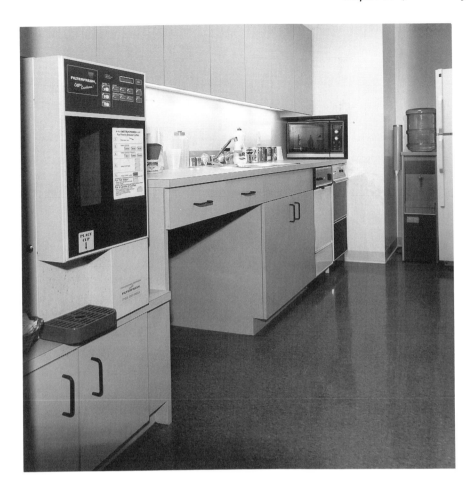

FIGURE 25.9
Kitchenette with accessible coffee maker and other appliances. Notice wide work space next to the sink with knee space. (The handles have been replaced with those originally specified by the architect.)

Before the renovation, many PVA staffers occupied cubicles opening on a corridor along the window wall (Figure 25.10). Aside from a lack of privacy and an environment not conducive for work, the open office layout wasted space. When the offices were re-designed the PVA figured it added 25% additional space for office uses that previously had been wasted space. The new private offices with modular furniture have accessible desks (able to accommodate two or more people in wheelchairs), accessible work surfaces, and accessible wall-mounted cabinets (Figure 25.11). Secretarial or executive assistant offices are smaller, but still designed with either modular or built-in accessible work surfaces and file drawers (Figures 25.12 and 25.13). In the rather small office of the executive assistant to the PVA's executive director, the double doors swing 180 degrees so that a person in a wheelchair can get into that office (Figure 25.14).

The office of the executive director, like those of the other senior managers, is large with the usual wooden furniture. But even with the most traditional style of desks, the knee space is high and wide enough to accommodate an executive in a wheelchair and additional accessible work space is built in along the wall (Figure 25.15).

FIGURE 25.10
Cubicle offices before renovation.

FIGURE 25.11
Private office of Jeff Dolezal, Director of
Training for Veterans Benefits, after
renovation showing accessible modular
furniture.

FIGURE 25.12
Low file cabinets with accessible countertop,
adjacent to secretary's desks.

FIGURE 25.13
Office has continuous knee space along two
walls.

Kim Beasley's pithy explanation for the limited seating provided at the 10th floor reception area: "people in wheelchairs bring
their own furniture" sums up the design philosophy for the PVA
renovation. Beasley and RTKL started with the premise that many
of the PVA workers and visitors would be using wheelchairs. By
contrast, most other designers on other projects imagine their

FIGURE 25.14
Double doors into small a office swing 180 degrees to provide a wide enough opening for someone in a wheelchair.

FIGURE 25.15
Executive director's office with built in accessible computer station along the wall. Notice the wide spaces for maneuvering a wheelchair.

spaces to be inhabited by nondisabled persons of average height and weight. For these designers, assuring accessibility is like any other code issue—something that has to be addressed, but not an element of the design statement. With the PVA renovation, all spaces and work areas were designed not to be minimally accessible, but easily accessible even if a particular office's occupant did not have a mobility disability. That the renovated spaces at the PVA are so dignified and attractive, not simply in comparison with their original appearances, should cause designers who do not see accessibility as compatible with high-quality design to rethink their views.

Chapter 26

HUBERT H. HUMPHREY PARK AND FRIENDSHIP HEIGHTS VILLAGE CENTER

Friendship Heights Village is a collection of new high-rise apartments/condominiums and exclusive stores serving an affluent community of somewhat more than 5000 people in an unincorporated special taxing area of 32 acres created by the Maryland General Assembly in 1914 and just over the border from the District of Columbia. In the midst of the village's expensive real estate is the Humphrey Park and the Friendship Heights Village Center, the latter completed in 1986. That same year the Maryland Society of the American Institute of Architects recognized the Friendship Heights Village Center with the society's Honor Award of Excellence. "A great functional plan, straightforward and complete inside and out. A handsome thoroughly resolved object built by a village council to a level of sophistication rarely seen from political clients." Designed by Walton Madden Cooper (Dennis Madden was architect of St. Elizabeth, see Chapter 18), the building should also be recognized for how successfully it relates to the older Humphrey Park completed in 1970 (designer unknown).

At the center of the Humphrey Park is a water fountain encircled by brick paths leading to the corners of the park. Three of the paths slope gently and only the fourth has steps (Figure 26.1). With streets forming the south, east, and north boundaries of the park, the village center building is the west boundary and its major space, the multipurpose room, is on an axis with the park's water fountain (Figure 26.2). The curved steps leading up to the doors of the gable-roofed multipurpose room continue the curve of the brick walkway surrounding the water fountain. From that walkway another curved brick path rises gently to the front door of the village center. Steps and a low ramp from the adjacent sidewalk also

FIGURE 26.1
Site plan of Friendship Heights Village
Center and Hubert H. Humphrey Park.
(From Walton Madden Cooper Inc.
Reproduced by permission.)

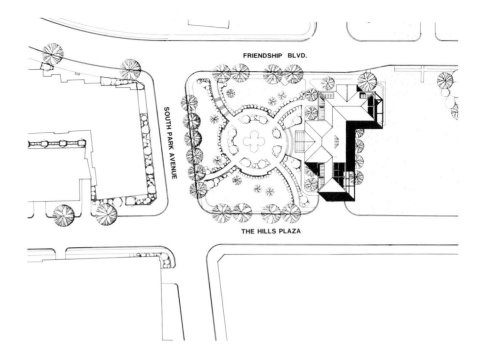

FIGURE 26.2
From Humphrey Park looking toward the
Village Center. Multipurpose room is at
center; main entrance is to the left in the
photograph. (Since this photograph was
taken a sculpture of a woman artist was
added near the fountain.)

lead to the building's main entrance (Figure 26.3). Both the ramp
and railings predate the ADA accessibility guidelines.

Once inside, the building's L-shaped floor plan is straightforward, readily comprehensible, and accessible with short, reasonably
wide corridors leading to all the rooms. The building's only steps or
stairs are those to the basement parking garage. Natural lighting
floods the building, especially the multipurpose room and the library. That room, with its magnifying glasses and strong portable
lamps for patrons with limited vision, is only space in the building

FIGURE 26.3
Steps and low ramp leading to the main entrance of Village Center and park. They predate the ADA accessibility guidelines and the only apparent changes have been to redo the curbcuts.

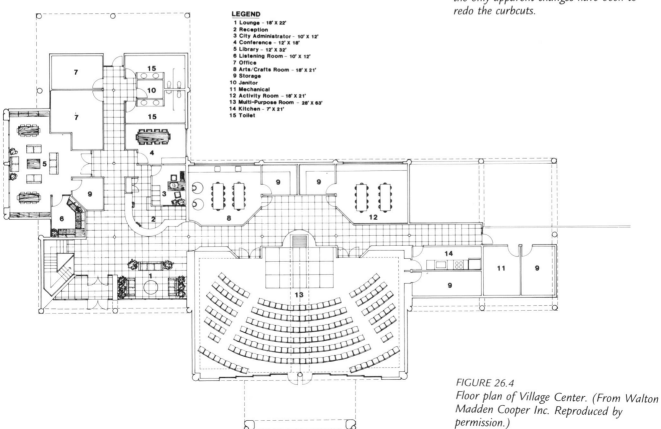

LEGEND
1 Lounge – 18' X 22'
2 Reception
3 City Administrator – 10' X 12'
4 Conference – 12' X 18'
5 Library – 12' X 32'
6 Listening Room – 10' X 12'
7 Office
8 Arts/Crafts Room – 18' X 21'
9 Storage
10 Janitor
11 Mechanical
12 Activity Room – 18' X 21'
13 Multi-Purpose Room – 28' X 63'
14 Kitchen – 7' X 21'
15 Toilet

FIGURE 26.4
Floor plan of Village Center. (From Walton Madden Cooper Inc. Reproduced by permission.)

that has additional accessibility features. In the rest of the building specific physical accessibility measures are limited to grab bars in the bathrooms and avoiding changes in elevation. But the simple layout and warm, natural lighting probably create an open, inviting and, therefore, emotionally accessible environment for people who, because of age or other mental disabilities, have trouble comprehending spatial relationships and are intimidated by government and other institutional buildings (Figure 26.4).

At the northwest corner of the building where the ramp leads to the parking garage, two ground-level spaces are reserved for cars having occupants with disabilities. From the reserved parking, a curb cut leads to a level path to the front door of the village center (Figure 26.5). Or the path can be taken to the water fountain either by the steps in front of the multipurpose room or by the brick path in front of the building's main entrance.

With its water fountain, numerous benches, chess tables, bronze sculpture of a woman sketching the village center (displayed at the 1992 United States Exposition in Seville, Spain; it was not at the park when the photograph was taken), beautifully sculpted plantings, and gently curving brick paths, the Humphrey Park is an inviting verdant retreat from the city and suburbia. With its comfortable scale, low massing, large expanses of glass panes, and visually interesting combination of gabled and hipped roofed pavilions, the village center is an equally inviting and quite unusual symbol and house of local government. With its layout and elevations relating so harmoniously to the park, the village center is the architectural complement of the park's landscape. The accessible paths of the park continue into the building to become its accessible corridors. Responding to the physical needs and emotional sensitivities of its affluent, largely ambulatory, and elderly citizenry, the Friendship Heights Village created a not overly ambitious civic complex of understated civility.

FIGURE 26.5
Reserved accessible parking on right. Curbcut and path at Village Center. Ramp to the basement garage is at extreme right edge of photograph.

Chapter 27

ACCESSIBLE PATHS TO OFFICES

Unless someone with a disability has an accessible path from a parking garage or the street to the office, the office remains inaccessible, regardless of its accessible features. In comparison with the path from the street to the office, the one from the underground parking garage to the office above is simple. For a building's garage to be accessible, the spaces must be tall and deep enough for a modified van and wide enough for a person in a wheelchair to get out of the vehicle (Figure 27.1). For some vehicles the modifications are limited to hand controls for the brakes and gas pedals whereas other vans have ramps and other special features (Figure

FIGURE 27.1
Van with lift at the back. Vans for people in wheelchairs often also have higher roofs than unmodified vans.

FIGURE 27.2
Van with ramp on the side. The van's owner can start the engine and have the ramp lowered by remote control. Once inside the van, all operations all operations can be controlled from the panel to the right of the driver's side. The lengths of the ramp necessitates a wide space next to a reserved parking space.

27.2). The reserved parking spaces for vehicles of people with disabilities should be adjacent to a low ramp to the elevator (Figure 27.3). In the elevator, the illuminated buttons should be properly labeled with braille and raised letters and within reach of someone in a wheelchair. Each floor should be announced audibly and visibly. At least that is what the ADA accessibility guidelines mandate.

The guidelines also detail the proper location, size, slope, and texture of street curbcuts. Placed at both sides of a corner intersection, the ADA-specified curbcuts have defined edges that alert people using canes that they are approaching a sloping cut in the

FIGURE 27.3
Ramp from accessible parking to elevators in Cambridge, MA office building.

sidewalk. On Washington, D.C.'s business corridor—K Street, N.W.—that type of curbcut is often at one side of the street and at the opposite side is a sloping curbcut that uses the entire corner of the sidewalk and lacks defined edges (Figures 27.4 and 27.5). In Boston's nineteenth-century manufacturing district near the waterfront, a curbcut and sidewalk were cleverly designed to eliminate steps from the street to the sidewalk to the accessible offices of the Adaptive Environments Center, a consultant on making facilities accessible (Figure 27.6). As the sidewalk's surface remains level rather than following the slope of the street, stairs are below instead of

FIGURE 27.4
On the near corner, two curbcuts. On the opposite corner, sloped curbcut. On the near corner, the change in color and surface from red brick to beige concrete provides warning to a person with limited or no vision that he or she is on the curbcut.

FIGURE 27.5
Sloped curbcut that occupies entire curve of the sidewalk. Lacking edge, change of surface, or change of color, the sloped curbcut provides no warning to the person with limited or no vision.

FIGURE 27.6
Boston sidewalk with curbcut. Rather than following the slope of the road, the sidewalk stays level so there are no steps from the sidewalk to the buildings.

FIGURE 27.7
The driveway and walkway to this building are on the same plane, so the bollards separate and protect pedestrians and people in wheelchairs from cars in the driveway.

above the sidewalk and bollards separate the stairs from the road. For a Washington, D.C. building, bollards separate the building's driveway from its walkway, protecting pedestrians and people in wheelchairs from cars (Figure 27.7).

Outside the new Washington, D.C. headquarters for the American Association of Retired Persons, the sidewalks (unlike the one in Boston) follow the slope of the streets; the building's corner entrance is level with the E Street sidewalk and below the grade of the 6th Street sidewalk. Architect Arthur May, FAIA, made the set of doors facing E Street automatic, controlled by a push plate. The other two sets of doors at the corner entrance are manual, and the doors facing 6th Street have stairs up to the street (Figures 27.8 and 27.9).

Another association headquartered in Washington, but dealing exclusively with the issue of disability is the National Organization on Disabilities, which recently moved to the Christian Science Church Building designed by I.M. Pei's office, on 16th Street, two blocks from the White House. Aside from its prestigious address,

FIGURE 27.8
American Association of Retired Persons building with main entrance at E and 6th Streets.

FIGURE 27.9
American Association of Retired Persons building. Automatic door with push plate control facing E Street.

FIGURE 27.10
Christian Science Church building and plaza to 16th Street.

the Christian Science Church building offered an accessible, level brick plaza to the building's entrance from 16th Street and a level, partially covered path from I Street where there are several parking lots and garages. At the entrance to the building, N.O.D. had the card scanner lowered to accommodate people in wheelchairs, but the manual, heavy doors remain difficult to open (Figures 27.10 and 27.11).

Around the corner from N.O.D., the Veterans Affairs building, under renovation to improve accessibility and other features, has sliding automatic doors controlled by a motion sensor at its temporary main entrance (Figure 27.12). In front of this entrance, the VA built a new landing approached by a long ramp on one side and stairs on the other (Figure 27.13).

FIGURE 27.11
Christian Science Church building and partially covered path to I Street.

FIGURE 27.12
Automatic sliding doors at temporary main entrance to the Veterans Affairs building.

FIGURE 27.13
Ramp at the Veterans Affairs. Note the wide curbcut at driveway in foreground. The curbcut has a defined edge only on the left side.

At the building that previously housed the United States Architectural and Transportation Barriers Compliance Board (Access Board), a motion sensor and lowered card scanner also controlled the automatic doors. But instead of the sliding doors at the VA, one door opened in as the other opened out at the Access Board (Figure 27.14). Since 1992, the Access Board, along with the President's

FIGURE 27.14
Former office building of the Access Board with automatic doors. As one door opens in, the other one opens out.

FIGURE 27.15
Midblock curbcuts in front of the Access Board building. Note that the curbcut in the foreground is partially obstructed. It is common for curbcuts to be blocked either by road construction materials or by parked vehicles.

Committee on the Employment of People with Disabilities, and the Justice Department's ADA compliance office have been at 1331 F Street, N.W., which has push plates rather than motion sensors controlling the two doors flanking the revolving door. In addition to curb cuts at both ends of the 1300 block of F Street, the District of Columbia installed midblock curbcuts in front of the entrance to the Access Board building and across the street. These additional curbcuts provide more direct accessible paths for the many workers and visitors in wheelchairs at 1331 F Street (Figure 27.15).

With new office buildings, like the AARP's and the Access Board's, the elevators are accessible in terms of size, signage, and position of buttons, but still lack audible announcements for each floor. For older buildings such as the Christian Science Church Building, braille and raised numerals are easily added to the control panels, but the buttons remain too high. A simple, yet clever solution was devised by the National Organization on Disabilities. A spring loaded handle enables someone who is short or in a wheelchair to push the button for N.O.D.'s sixth floor office (Figures 27.16 and 27.17).

Only when they are more common and have had greater use by people with disabilities and the nondisabled will it become apparent which type of curbcut, automatic door, or elevator modification is preferable. Only with greater usage will the need for further refinements be identified. (For example, if corner curbcuts are proven to be a hazard for people with limited or no vision, what tactile surface warning is needed? See Figure 27.18.)

FIGURE 27.16
Elevator panel at the Christian Science building, with handle for pushing the sixth floor button to the left. N.O.D. occupies the sixth floor.

FIGURE 27.17
Elevator panel at the Christian Science building, with the handle for the sixth floor button engaged.

FIGURE 27.18
Silver Spring, MD metro station. Raised
bumps and color change warn blind and
visually impaired pedestrians that they are
on the curbcut.

Chapter 28

GREAT HALL AT THE DEPARTMENT OF JUSTICE BUILDING

In 1991, then Attorney General Richard Thornburgh led his department in celebrating the first anniversary of the signing of the Americans with Disabilities Act in the Department of Justice's Great Hall. Although the room and its stage were already accessible, the Great Hall was renovated before the July 26 ceremony, substantially improving its accessibility and appearance.

Built from 1931 to 1934 to the design of Zantzinger, Borie and Medary, the Department of Justice building occupies one of Washington, D.C.'s most prominent sites midway between the Capitol and the White House. Filling the entire block defined by 10th Street on the west, Constitution Avenue on the south, 9th Street on the east, and Pennsylvania Avenue on the north, the building is a truncated rectangle with its main facade angled to follow the diagonal of Pennsylvania Avenue. A substantial interior courtyard, with an entrance from 10th Street, runs west to east. Two smaller courtyards are south of the large interior courtyard and are separated by a major wing of the building which runs south from the interior courtyard to the rear (Constitution Avenue) wing of the building. At the courtyard entrance to this wing, the cobblestone drive slopes up to the sidewalk, providing access without altering the handsome stone curb and sidewalk (Figure 28.1).

Just inside the courtyard entrance, curved staircases lead to the second floor landing. Up four more steps is the Great Hall (Figure 28.2). At the far end of the room, which runs the length of the north—south corridor separating the two smaller interior courtyards, more steps go up to the elevator lobby/corridor of the building's Constitution Avenue wing. As neither end of the Great Hall is accessible, a path for people in wheelchairs was created going through an office northwest of the Great Hall and down a chair lift into the antechamber west of the Great Hall. A curtain wall with aluminum sash windows and automatic doors separates the antechamber from the Great Hall. To get to the stage of the Great Hall,

FIGURE 28.1
Courtyard of the Justice Department building with sloped driveway up to stone curb and sidewalk. The Great Hall is on the second floor.

FIGURE 28.2
Steps up to the Great Hall from the lobby north of the room.

someone in a wheelchair had to use a chair lift, variously described as rickety, noisy, and shaky.

In view of Attorney General Thornburgh's personal interest in the Americans with Disabilities Act, it was inevitable that the Department celebrate the first anniversary of the bill's signing.

> As a parent of a disabled child, as a former Governor, and as Attorney General, I have witnessed the many faces of discrimination confronting persons with disabilities. It is therefore particularly satisfying for me to have been a part of the effort to remove our society's barriers to persons with disabilities. The elimination of these barriers—attitudinal, architectural, and communications barriers—will enable all of us to benefit from the skills and talents of persons with disabilities and will enable persons with disabilities to lead more productive lives [*Worklife*, Fall 1990, volume 3, number 3].

Given the awkwardness of the Great Hall's accessible path it was also inevitable that it would be renovated before the ADA anniversary ceremony. Thornburgh and his wife, Ginny, a long-time advocate of the rights of people with disabilities, were especially bothered by the lift to the stage which called undue attention to the user and meant that people with disabilities used one method and the nondisabled used a different one—steps—to get to the stage. The Thornburghs believed strongly that the goal of equal access/universal design required one means for everyone to get to the stage. It was also awkward that people in wheelchairs went through workers' offices to get to the Great Hall.

Justice Department Architect Anna Young Franz, AIA, consulted with the department's accessibility task force, the General Service Administration's historic preservationists (GSA is landlord for all federal government buildings), Amy Weinstein, AIA, and Jane Barton, curator of the U.S. Department of Treasury building (the latter two brought in by Mrs. Thornburgh), and then submitted several proposals for improved accessibility in the Great Hall. Under the plan implemented, the workers were moved out of the office that the original accessible path went through. That space is now used exclusively as the entrance to the path to the Great Hall (Figures 28.3 and 28.4). That route, which meets the Uniform Federal Accessibility Standards for width, could not be widened as its walls are loadbearing. The chair lift from the former office to the Great Hall's antechamber was replaced with a ramp (Figure 28.5). From the antechamber someone in a wheelchair uses either of the automatic doors controlled by a push plate to enter the Great Hall (Figure 28.6).

At the Great Hall's stage, the stairs and chair lift were replaced with two ramps. Each ramp is flanked by low walls with handrails mounted near the top of each wall. All people now enter and exit the stage the same way. To simulate the stone walls of the Great Hall, the sheetrock walls and stage fascia were faux painted (Figure 28.7). Carl Paul Jennewein's streamlined, aluminum sculptures flanking the stage's curtains (Spirit of Justice on the left and the

FIGURE 28.3
View from former office to the upper part of
the accessible ramp to Great Hall's
antechamber.

FIGURE 28.4
View from accessible ramp toward the
former office. Windows to the interior
courtyard are on the left and a window into
an inactive elevator shaft is on the right.

FIGURE 28.5
View from the antechamber up the lower
part of the ramp. Two push plates for
automatic doors to the Great Hall are
visible on the right and rear walls.

FIGURE 28.6
From the Great Hall's stage toward the curtain wall separating the Great Hall from the antechamber. The north corridor is to the right (see Figure 28.2).

Majesty of Law) inspired the shape and color of the ramps' handrails. More permanent materials were not used for the ramps and stage as the building is to undergo extensive and expensive renovations, which will also improve accessibility, starting in 1996.

One of Franz's earlier plans for the Great Hall proposed that the ramp to the antechamber be sloped more gradually and continue through the antechamber's curtain wall to the stage. This plan was rejected, partly on historic preservation grounds, as it would have substantially altered the curtain wall. After reviewing Franz's final, implemented plan, the Justice Department's accessibility task force, which has members who use wheelchairs, recommended that stairs to the stage between the ramps be added. Some accessibility experts contend that people with certain visual and other disabilities can use stairs more easily and safely than they can ramps. The accessibility task force's recommendation was rejected, in part, because adding steps would have further reduced the number of seats, already too few, in the Great Hall. Both proposals were also unac-

FIGURE 28.7
Elevated view of the Great Hall.

ceptable because they did not satisfy the Thornburghs' position that equal access/universal design required one approach for all to the stage. (For a stage with ramps and stairs see Judith Resnik School, Chapter 7.)

As a grand circulation hall serving as a grand auditorium, the Great Hall had serious inadequacies. It had limited seating, poor sight lines, and an awkward accessible path with a noisy, distracting, perhaps unsafe, chair lift to the stage. Designs to improve the Great Hall's accessibility had to address the planned building renovation, historic preservation concerns, the need for the maximum number of seats, and the Thornburghs' views on universal design. (On the other hand, if the Attorney General had not been personally interested, it is unlikely that an office would have been freed up to become the entrance to the accessible path.) Despite or probably because of all the factors influencing the renovation, the Great Hall now has the presence and grandeur it previously lacked.

Chapter 29

UNITED STATES CAPITOL

Despite its preeminence as a national symbol, tourist attraction, and office building, the Capitol has limited accessibility.* This incongruity was not lost on Senator John McCain when he addressed his fellow senators on March 3, 1992:

> Mr. President, on January 26, 1992, the Americans with Disabilities Act mandated the removal of physical barriers in public and commercial facilities to promote access for the disabled. As one of the authors of that landmark act, I am calling on the Committee on Rules and Administration to promulgate and institute new guidelines to ensure that the Senate is in full compliance with the law of the land. . . . The current situation is an egregious example of the Senate once again setting separate, much more lenient, standards for itself than we have imposed on the remainder of society. We must rectify this situation.

Efforts to make accessible the Capitol (House as well as Senate side), the Senate and House Office buildings, the Supreme Court, and the Library of Congress, all under the purview of the Architect of the Capitol, date at least as far back as 1973. That year, Edward Noakes, architectural consultant and chairman of the President's Committee on the Handicapped was retained to conduct an accessibility survey of the Capitol, its buildings, and grounds. The Architect of the Capitol, George White, FAIA, commissioned the study. He then requested and the Congress appropriated funds in fiscal year 1976 to implement Noakes's recommendations. Between 1976 and the end of 1992, while White's office carried out the recommendations, another three accessibility surveys were conducted. One was by Ron Mace, FAIA, for Senator John East, who used a wheelchair, another by the Access Board at the request of then Vice

---

*Started in the late eighteenth century and essentially completed in the mid-nineteenth century, the Capitol was designed and refined by William Thornton, Benjamin Henry Latrobe, Charles Bulfinch, Robert Mills, and Thomas Ustick Walter. The current east front was created in 1959–1960. Cass Gilbert designed the Supreme Court, which was built in 1935.

President Dan Quayle, who had offices at the Capitol, and the last (and just completed) by Robert Lynch, AIA for the Architect of the Capitol.

Physical changes and new services to improve accessibility, while benefitting both visitors and workers with disabilities seemed directed more for visitors. A certain number of ramps, both temporary and permanent, were added, and some water fountains, bathrooms, telephones, and door openings were modified to be accessible. Also, text telephones were added in offices and at some pay telephones. But the major accessibility feature was probably the creation of the Special Services for Disabled Visitors office, in the crypt of the Capitol. Special service employees give tours of the Capitol, but only for tourists with disabilities. Those with visual disabilities are encouraged to touch the statues, like the one of Robert Fulton who holds a miniature steamboat on his lap (Figure 29.1). Descriptions of the sights along the tour are available in braille text and the tour guide accompanies her commentary with sign language for tourists who have hearing disabilities. Also, these tours are along a route accessible to someone in a wheelchair. To further aid visitors, three dimensional tactile models of the Capitol and the buildings on the Mall are displayed in the crypt near the Special Services office. (Only the front part of the office is accessible because of steps, so even that service could not employ someone who uses a wheelchair.)

Also available to tourists with visual disabilities is a series of five tactile maps by University of Maryland Professor Joseph Wiedel. Funded by the Department of Education, the maps were conceived by George Covington, on detail to the Department of Education, and then reassigned to Speaker of the House Jim Wright's office so that he could assure that the project was promptly completed in late 1987. Three maps detail the floors of the Capitol while another shows the Mall from the Capitol to the Washington Monument; and the last map is from the Washington Monument to Arlington National Cemetery. Wiedel, who was the first chairman of the Commission on Tactual and Low Vision Mapping of the International Cartographic Association, also prepared Gallaudet University's tactile map (see Chapter 6), advised the National Building Museum on its permanent exhibition (see Chapter 13), and was consultant to the National Park Service on its accessibility maps (see Chapter 14), among his numerous other activities pertaining to cartographic aids for people with visual disabilities. Wiedel used various textures on the Capitol maps, together with contrasting colors and braille to indicate building features, such as the columns at the center of the crypt, private offices, and public spaces. The private offices, for example, are rendered in blue/gray and have a cross-hatched texture, whereas the corridors and public rooms, such as the Old Supreme Court, are white with a smooth surface. The columns in the crypt are in a public space so they are represented as raised bumps on a white background. The grounds of the Capitol are represented in pale green with a pebble texture (Figure 29.2).

FIGURE 29.1
United States Capitol, National Statuary Hall. Sculpture of New Yorker Robert Fulton holding one of his inventions, the steamboat. Tourists with visual disabilities like to touch the steamboat.

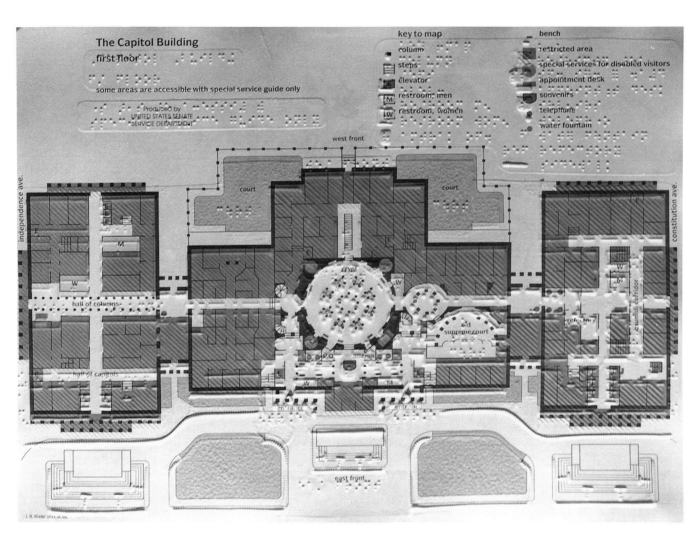

FIGURE 29.2
Tactile map of the first floor of the Capitol.
Contrasting colors and textures are used in
addition to the text and braille.

FIGURE 29.3
Capitol, south end. Temporary ramp up to
the portico entrance.

FIGURE 29.4
Capitol, south end, newly installed ramped floor of portico.

At the north and south entrances to the Capitol and at the entrance to the Supreme Court, the Architect of the Capitol initially had wooden ramps installed over the steps (Figure 29.3). The temporary ramps and permanent steps at the side entrances to the Capitol have been removed and the porticos that the stairs/ramps led up to have been redone as accessible ramps (Figure 29.4). At the Supreme Court, the wooden ramp over the steps to the terrace was removed and a chair lift was cut into the wall of the terrace (Figures 29.5–29.7). That chair lift is apparently the only exterior one in Washington,D.C. not requiring a key; the only other keyless one is inside the Vice President's residence (see Chapter 30). The Supreme Court chair lift will be removed once a permanent ramp is completed. At the entrance to the building, a metal ramp with a textured surface and handrails abuts the one step (Figure 29.8).

That the Architect of the Capitol fully appreciates the architectural, historical, and symbolic importance of the Capitol and the other buildings on Capitol Hill is apparent in the deliberate, slow fashion that accessibility features are added and in their careful design. As seen in the ramps added inside the Capitol, no detail is overlooked (Figures 29.9 and 29.10).

In an effort to get the Architect of the Capitol moving faster on accessibility, Senator Robert Dole wrote to him on December 4,

FIGURE 29.5
Supreme Court. Steps to left previously had
been temporarily ramped. Stair lift is cut
into the terrace wall at right.

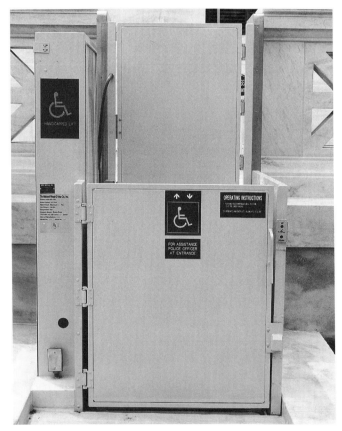

FIGURE 29.6
Chair lift, note curb details which make the
lift appear to be an integral part of the
terrace wall and approach.

FIGURE 29.7
Terrace side of chair lift. Note the raised
surface and sloping sides of the ramp.

FIGURE 29.8
Metal ramp to entrance to Supreme Court.

FIGURE 29.9
Capitol, permanent interior ramp.

FIGURE 29.10
Capitol. Long ramp over stairs. The balustrade is designed to look original to the late-eighteenth-, early-nineteenth-century building interior.

1984: "The Capitol of the United States continues to represent government of the people, by the people, and for the people to persons around the world. Every effort to make it fully accessible to all of America's citizens is surely in order." Only with a sensitivity raised by the passage of the Americans with Disabilities Act and the prodding of some members of Congress has the Office of the Architect of the Capitol moved from what it described as a reactive to a proactive position on making the Capitol and the related buildings fully accessible. The appropriateness of the accessibility changes made by the Architect of the Capitol should inspire other designers making accessible other old, but not nearly as stellar buildings.

Chapter 30

VICE PRESIDENT'S RESIDENCE

A massive, 100-year-old building, the vice president's house possesses some attractive details, but lacks the architectural quality of its neighbors such as the British Embassy's outstanding building by Sir Edward Lutyens. And directly south of and on higher ground than the vice president's residence is a distinguished classical revival building by Richard Morris Hunt. With a circular library at one end and an observatory for a 12-inch telescope at the other end, Hunt's building is the centerpiece of nine buildings he designed for the nearly 100-acre grounds of the Naval Observatory. The vice president's residence was designed by a local Washington, D.C. architect, Leon Dessez, to be the home of the superintendent of the Naval Observatory. In 1974, the house was designated the official

FIGURE 30.1
Front of the Vice President's residence. Guard's building is to left.

FIGURE 30.2
*Rear of the Vice President's residence
showing curbcut and ramp to the entrance.*

vice presidential residence. The front entrance to the vice president's house is inaccessible, as there are stairs from the porte-cochere to the porch and then another step to the front door (Figure 30.1).

Since October 1991, the residence's public and main entrance has been the renovated, accessible rear doors. Alan Meyers, AIA, gutted and expanded a 1930s rear wing addition to the house's first floor to create, according to the Uniform Federal Accessibility Standards, an accessible path into and through the first floor.

The route starts with a new curbcut at the circular drive, behind the house, where visitors are dropped off. From the sidewalk a short path leads to the ramp which wraps around the side of the rear wing to the stair landing in front of the rear doors. The route taken by people using the ramp is, therefore, only slightly longer and nearly as direct as the route up the stairs (Figures 30.2 and 30.3).

The rear entrance opens onto a relatively wide corridor which goes past some offices and then turns right. Along this second short corridor are the doors to the accessible men's and women's

FIGURE 30.3
Victor McCoy, Sr., president of Paralyzed Veterans of America, approaches the ramp. Notice handrail extension of ramp 1 foot past the ramp. Although the railing stops at the building, the handrail continues, so that there is a handrail on both sides of the ramp.

bathrooms. Having round doorknobs, loose floor rugs, and handles that are not levered, the bathrooms are not as accessible as they should be. But one sink in each bathroom has generous knee space beneath it for someone in a wheelchair. If both sinks were accessible, they would not suggest separate but equal facilities (Figure 30.4).

Beyond the bathrooms, a tight left turn leads to the stairs up to the first floor of the vice president's residence. A compact chair lift, costing $20,000 (which is what it cost to build the house in 1893), provides access over the stairs. The lift is controlled by the person using it and does not require an attendant either to unlock it or operate it (Figures 30.5–30.7).

As no member of the vice president's family or, presumably, his household staff had a mobility disability, the accessible route is limited to the first floor, the only floor where the public is entertained.

When Vice President Quayle and his wife first realized that their official residence was inaccessible, they had four options:

FIGURE 30.4
*Bathroom with accessible knee space below
one sink, with less accessible features of
knob on door, nonlever handle, and loose
floor rug.*

FIGURE 30.5
Victor McCoy operating wheelchair lift.

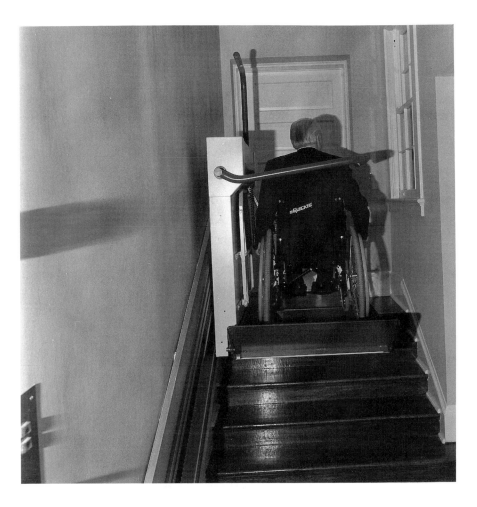

FIGURE 30.6
McCoy leaving wheelchair lift. The front bar has been raised out of the way. Notice additional safety features of rear bar and bottom panel that angles up. Controls to summon the lift are along the wall at the extreme left edge of the photograph.

FIGURE 30.7
Wheelchair lift folded against the wall. Notice plant holder at corner, further reducing the already tight wheelchair maneuvering space.

1. Do nothing because no one was going to force them to make changes, regardless of legal requirements.
2. Leave the front door as the inaccessible main public entrance and create an accessible back public entrance.
3. Make the front entrance accessible.
4. Make the back door the accessible public entrance.

To have altered the porte-cochere and front door to make them accessible would have damaged the building's historic fabric (although it has never been designated a landmark). By making the newly accessible rear entrance the only public entrance, the vice president, practically and symbolically, made access to the house equal for all members of the public and preserved a separate, private front entrance just for the vice president's family use.

Chapter 31

UNITED STATES EQUAL EMPLOYMENT OPPORTUNITY COMMISSION

Under the Civil Rights Act of 1964, the EEOC was created to enforce provisions against hiring discrimination based on the applicant's race, color, religion, sex, or national origin. In the ensuing years, the definition of discriminated groups was expanded to include the aged and the disabled—and the responsibilities of the EEOC were also increased. The Americans with Disabilities Act of 1990 solidified 26 years of federal laws, executive orders, and reorganization plans concerning employment discrimination and assigned to the EEOC responsibility for Title I of the Act—Employment.

To consolidate its Washington, D.C. headquarters staff into one building, the EEOC signed a lease in 1988 to be sole tenant of a 10 story, approximately 160,000 square foot office building. Because the 1801 L Street, N.W. building was nearly complete, the EEOC's interior designer, Leo A Daly (Lida Desoorkian, IBD, project manager), was limited to achieving an accessible work environment by designing the office layout and specifying furniture, rather than by making structural or even floor and wall surface changes. The EEOC managers handed the Leo A Daly team a copy of the Uniform Federal Accessibility Standards to assure that the design was accessible. The EEOC moved in in 1990.

The first floor guard's desk at the EEOC building has high and low counters so that someone who is short or in a wheelchair can sign in (Figure 31.1). From the guard's desk an accessible path leads to the elevators (with illuminated buttons and braille and raised floor numbers) and to the commission's training facility. A second accessible path from the building's rear door leads to the training center, enabling a person in a wheelchair to park and get out of a van in the alley instead of in front of the building in heavy traffic. In the training center's kitchen an oven and a dishwasher, both with accessible front controls, flank a counter with an accessible food preparation area and sink. Clear knee space runs the length

FIGURE 31.1
U.S. Equal Employment Opportunity Commission, 1801 L Street, NW. Guard desk with counters at two heights.

of the counter and the pipes are padded or recessed, except for the garbage disposal. The garbage disposal control is accessible, mounted on the front panel of the counter (Figure 31.2).

The EEOC's library is as accessible as the kitchen. The library's aisles, information desk, card catalogue, and reading tables are wheelchair accessible, and the doors to the library are controlled by push panel automatic doors (a feature recently added to the bathrooms). For library users with limited vision, several types of machines are available to magnify text.

The bathrooms, however, do not entirely comply with the Uniform Federal Accessibility Standards. Although the sinks have lever handles and clear knee space (Figure 31.3), the toilet stalls lack the second, rear grab bar. A senior ADA expert at the EEOC said that if anyone had complained during the 2 years the agency has occupied the building, the rear grab bar would have been installed immediately.

Constructing an accessible bathroom according to Uniform Federal Accessibility Standards was also a problem at the Presi-

FIGURE 31.2
Kitchen with accessible controls on oven, garbage disposal, and dishwasher; padded or recessed pipes; and lever handles. The work surface to the left of the sink and the sink have clear knee space under them.

FIGURE 31.3
EEOC bathroom sink with two lever handles, knee space running the length of the counter, and recessed pipes.

dent's Committee on the Employment of People with Disabilities which moved into new quarters 10 blocks from the EEOC in mid-1992. There the bathroom counter had the correct clearance, but the top of the counter was too high for someone in a wheelchair or who is short to use the single lever control (different from the two levers at EEOC bathroom) or soap dispenser. After mod-

FIGURE 31.4
President's Committee on the Employment of People with Disabilities, 1331 F Street, NW. Bathroom. Clear knee space is at the right height, but the top of the counter was too high so the section to the right has a lower top. Single lever handle used. Note that Uniform Federal Accessibility Standards for sinks provide clearance for someone in a wheelchair, but not in a battery-powered cart used by Mr. Richard Sheppard of the President's Committee. He approaches the sink at an angle.

FIGURE 31.5
EEOC work station. Wall cabinets can be positioned at different heights to suit the office occupant.

FIGURE 31.6
EEOC attorney Deidre Davis in her office. She can wheel under the desk tops to her left and she can reach the cabinet or the work surfaces in front by wheeling parallel to them. Although her work space seems tight it is better than some of her colleagues', which are too small for her to wheel into.

ifications, one sink in each bathroom at the President's Committee has a counter top at the proper height (Figure 31.4).

In EEOC's offices, such as attorney Deidre Davis's, the layout of the modular furniture appears tight, but she has room to maneuver, and she can reach items in the hanging cabinet and on work surfaces. Also the modular work surfaces are high enough for her to wheel her chair into the knee spaces. Mounted on tracks, the wall cabinets in Ms. Davis's and other offices can be set at different heights to suit the occupant. Although the EEOC office spaces are supposedly more generous than the General Service Administration's standards (specifying square footage based on grade level), Ms. Davis said there was not room for her to confer in the smaller offices of some of her colleagues (Figures 31.5 and 31.6).

Not all offices at the EEOC are designed around modular wall units. Attorney Christopher Bell's more traditional looking office is cluttered with papers and machines. He has a scanner which reads aloud the text it is viewing and another machine which displays a substantially enlarged version of the text placed beneath its lens.

FIGURE 31.7
EEOC attorney Christopher Bell in his more traditional work space. To the extreme left is a scanner connected to the computer, which reads aloud the document being scanned. His computer monitor is mounted so that he can get close enough to read the screen. Mr. Bell is working at a display that greatly enlarges the type on the document he is holding.

Also, his computer monitor is mounted on a high stand at the front edge of his desk so that he can get very close to the screen to read it (Figure 31.7).

Evan Kemp, the EEOC's chairman, also prefers a more traditional office. But his large wooden executive desk is raised on a base so that he can wheel into the knee space, and the door to his office is controlled by high-tech push panel and card scanner mounted on a modular wall panel. When pressed, the push panel automatically opens the door; the scanner controls access after normal business hours. During the work day the door can be opened manually by its lever handle (Figure 31.8).

The Commission's hearing room was also designed to accommodate Mr. Kemp and others in wheel chairs. At the commissioners' table, reached by a short low ramp, the microphone for Mr. Kemp is at the front edge of the table so he does not have to reach forward to use it. At the rear of the hearing room is an outside balcony that was inaccessible as designed, but made accessible by

FIGURE 31.8
Entrance to the EEOC chairman's office.
On the modular wall to the left are the
button to automatically open the door and
the card scanner controlling access after
hours. Mr. Kemp's traditional executive
wooden desk has been raised on a wooden
plinth so that he has sufficient clearance at
the desk's knee space. Both doors have lever
handles.

FIGURE 31.9
EEOC hearing room. Note the short, low
ramp to the commissioner's table.

FIGURE 31.10
EEOC hearing room. Commissioners' table with microphone at the front edge of the table so that Mr. Kemp will not have to reach forward to use it.

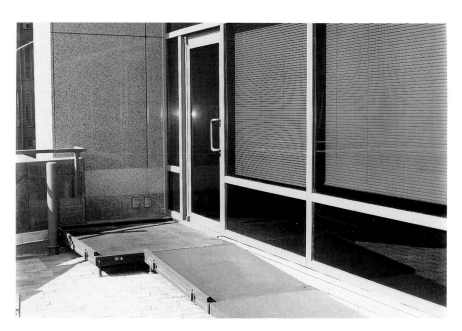

FIGURE 31.11
EEOC balcony off hearing room. Retrofitted ramp with textured surface has a wide platform in front of the door for maneuvering a wheelchair. Without the ramp, the balcony, which is approximately one step down, would be inaccessible.

the installation of a metal ramp with a textured surface. The ramp's wide platform in front of the door provides maneuvering space for a person in a wheelchair (Figures 31.9–31.12).

As they should be, the EEOC offices are models of accessibility. But certain features raise important issues. Why has no EEOC employee in a wheelchair complained that the bathroom's rear grab bar was absent? Either the Uniform Federal Accessibility Standards (and ADA accessibility guidelines) go too far or even people with disabilities at the EEOC are afraid to complain about barriers. That a straightforward accessibility standard could be overlooked at the

EEOC reiterates the importance of contractors *and* clients not only knowing the accessibility standards, but understanding the underlying rationale. Also, how should the General Service Administration's or any employer's space standards be reconciled to the apparently more generous accessibility standards? Should every work space be big enough to accommodate someone in a wheelchair or only when it is the primary work space of someone in a wheelchair? Finally, as assistive technology—whether it is computer hardware or software, scanner, automatic door, telephone headset cradle, or modified elevator button—becomes even more common at the EEOC and other offices, enabling more people with disabilities to work in offices, perhaps for the first time, how will office architecture and design best accommodate assistive technology?

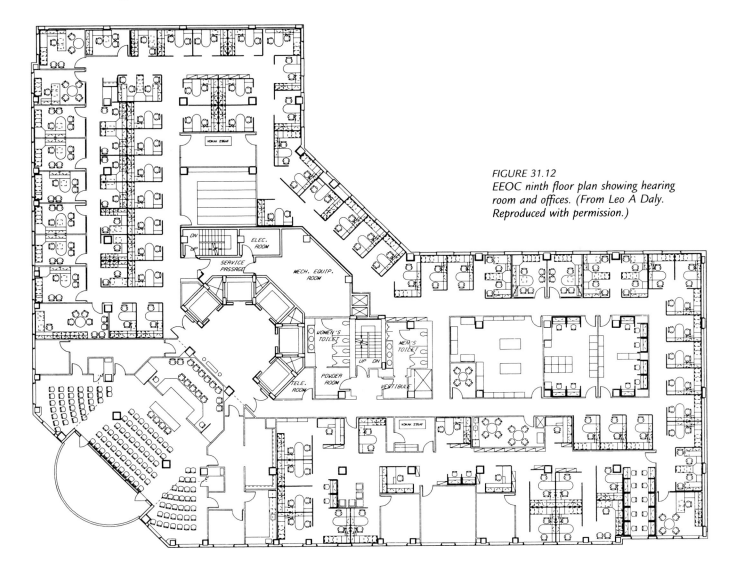

FIGURE 31.12
EEOC ninth floor plan showing hearing room and offices. (From Leo A Daly. Reproduced with permission.)

INFORMATION SOURCES

Copies of the ADA legislation and regulations can be obtained by calling the Justice Department's ADA Information Line or the Access Board's telephone. The Access Board will also provide copies of the *Uniform Federal Accessibility Standard* (FED-STD-795, April 1, 1988) and the Access Board's various studies. As it is difficult to get through to either the Justice Department or Access Board telephone numbers, an alternative way of finding the relevant legislation and regulations would be to go to a larger public library or law library having the *United States Statutes at Large*, published yearly by the U.S. Government Printing Office, and the *Federal Register*. The former provides the text of legislation, but the reader needs to know what year the legislation was passed. The latter prints all government regulations. Copies of current legislation can be obtained by writing the House Document Room, U.S. House of Representatives, Washington, DC 20515 or the Senate Document Room, U.S. Senate, Washington, DC 20510. The *Federal Register* is published by the National Archives and Records Administration, Washington, DC 20408.

Americans with Disabilities Act is Public Law 101-336. Its citation in *United States Statutes at Large* is 104 STAT. 328.

Fair Housing Amendments Act of 1988 is Public Law 100-430. Its citation in *United States Statutes at Large* is 102 STAT. 1619.

Rehabilitation Act of 1973, as amended, is Public Law 93-112. Its citation in *United States Statutes at Large* is 87 STAT. 355.

Abrams, A. Jay and Abrams, Margaret Ann. *The First Whole Rehab Catalog: A Comprehensive Guide to Products and Services for the Physically Disadvantaged.* Crozet, VA: Betterway Publications, Inc., 1991.

Adaptive Environments Center, Inc., 374 Congress St., Suite 301, Boston, MA 02210, (617) 695-1225 (V/TDD), (617) 482-8099 (FAX). Conducts training on ADA, Fair Housing, and Section 504 and produces and distributes several publications on accessible design.

Airport Operators Council, Inc., 12220 19th St., NW, Suite 200, Washington, DC 20036, (202) 293-8500, *A Guide to Accessibility of Terminals,* ACCESS TRAVEL; AIRPORTS, 6th edition, August 1991, with assistance of United States Office of Consumer Affairs and American Academy of Otolaryngology, Head & Neck Surgery. Report prepared by Corporate Services for the Deaf, Inc., 1661 E. Camelback, Suite 250, Phoenix, Arizona 85016, (602) 230-7940.

Alexander Graham Bell Association for the Deaf, 3417 Volta Place, NW, Washington, DC 20007-2778, (202) 337-5220 (TDD/V).

American Association for the Advancement of Science, Project on Science, Technology and Disability, 1333 H St., NW, Washington, DC 20005, (202) 326-6670. List of Publications, June 1991.

American Association of Retired Persons, 601 E St., NW, Washington, DC 20049, (202) 434-2277:
Product Report: Wheelchairs, Vol. 1, No. 5, Oct. 1990.
Product Report: Hearing Aids, Vol. 1, No. 4, Dec. 1989.
A Change for the Better: How to Make Communities More Responsive to Older Residents, 1989 (authors: Valerie Parker, Sherry Edmonds, Virginia Robinson).
The Do-able Renewable Home: Making Your Home Fit Your Needs, 1985 (author: John P.S. Salmen). *See also* Universal Designers & Consultants.

American Foundation for the Blind, 15 West 16th St., New York, NY 10011, (800) 232-5463, (212) 620-2000. Publication Catalog, 1991-1992.

American Hotel & Motel Association, 1201 New York Ave., NW, Washington, DC 20005, (202) 289-3100. *Accommodating All Guests: The Americans with Disabilities Act and the Lodging Industry,* 1992 (author: John P. S. Salmen). *See also* Universal Designers & Consultants.

American Institute of Architects, 1735 New York Ave., NW, Washington, DC 20036. Professional Development Assessment Program, (202) 626-7479:
ADA Searchware: Reference Software for the Americans with Disabilities Act.
The ADA Accessibility Kit.
ADA: A Resource Guide.
ADA Client Brochures.
BOMA International ADA Compliance Guidebook. See Building Owners and Managers Association International.
"National Resources on Employing People with Disabilities" (handout prepared by AIA Library which has other holdings pertaining to accessible design).

American National Standards Institute, 11 West 42nd St., New York, NY 10036. For ANSI A117.1-1992, the Secretariat was the Council of American Buildings Officials, 5203 Leesburg Pike, Suite 708, Falls Church, VA. 22041, (703) 931-4533. Copies of the Standard can be purchased from the Council or at certain bookstores such as the AIA Bookstore.

Barrier free Environments, Inc., P. O. Box 30634, Water Garden, Highway 70 West, Raleigh, NC 27622, (919) 782-7823, (919) 787-1984 (FAX). *The Accessible Housing Design File.* New York: Van Nostrand Reinhold, 1991. Barrier free Environments has written several other books.

Branson, Gary D., *The Complete Guide to Barrier-Free Housing: Convenient Living for the Elderly and Physically Handicapped.* Crozet, VA: Betterway Publications, Inc., 1991.

Building Owners and Managers Association (BOMA) International, 1201 NY Ave., NW, Suite 300, Washington, DC 20005, (202) 408-2662, (202) 371-0181 (FAX). *BOMA International's ADA Compliance Guidebook: A Checklist for Your Building: Meeting the Title #/Provisions of the Americans with Disabilities Act: Public Accommodations and Commercial Facilities*, 1991. Now distributed by the AIA.

Dole Foundation for Employment of Persons with Disabilities, 1819 H St., NW, Suite 850, Washington, DC 20006, (202) 457-0318.

Evan Terry Associates, P.C., *Americans with Disabilities Act Facilities Compliance Workbook*. New York: Wiley, 1992. Looseleaf book that will be supplemented periodically.

Grey House Publishing, Inc., 1992: *The Complete Directory for People with Disabilities*. Detroit: Gale Research, 1991.

Helen Keller National Center for Deaf-Blind Youths and Adults, 111 Middle Neck Rd., Sands Point, NY 11050, (516) 944-8900 (V/TDD). Has several handouts on adapting environments for people who are visually and hearing disabled.

JOB Accommodation Network, 809 Allen Hall, West Virginia University, P.O. Box 6122, Morgantown, WV 26506-6122, (800) JAN-7234, (304) 293-7186. JAN answers callers' questions concerning making accommodations for employees with disabilities.

Lifchez, Raymond. *Rethinking Architecture: Design Students and Physically Disabled People*. Berkeley: University of California Press, 1987.

Maryland Technology Assistance Program, Office for Individuals with Disabilities, One Market Center, 300 West Lexington Street, Box 10, Baltimore, MD 21201-3435, (410) 339-4975 (V/TDD), (410) 333-6674 (FAX), SpecialNet: MD.TECH.HQ.

Museum of Science. *New Dimensions for Traditional Dioramas: Multisensory Additions for Access, Interest and Learning*. Boston, 1991 (author: Betty Davidson).

Mueller, James, *The Workplace Workbook: An Illustrated Guide to Job Accommodation and Assistive Technology*. Washington, DC: The Dole Foundation, 1990. *See also* National Rehabilitation Hospital.

Muscular Dystrophy Association, 810 Seventh Ave., New York, NY 10019, (212) 586-0808.

NAHB National Research Center, 400 Prince George's Boulevard, Upper Marlboro, MD 20772-8731, (301) 249-4000, (301) 249-3096 (FAX). Publications on adapting housing for people with disabilities.

National Easter Seal Society, 70 East Lake St., Chicago, IL. 60601, (312) 726-6200, (312) 243-8880 (TDD).

National Federation of the Blind, 1800 Johnson St., Baltimore, MD 21230, (410) 659-9314.

National Information Center on Deafness, Gallaudet University, 800 Florida Ave., NE, Washington, DC 20002-3695, (202) 651-5051 (V), (202) 651-5052 (TDD). Several publications pertaining to deafness.

National Multiple Sclerosis Society, 205 East 42nd St., 3rd Floor, New York, New York 10017, (800) 624-2836, (212) 986-3240.

National Organization on Disability (N.O.D.), 910 16th St., NW, Washington, DC 20006, (202) 293-5960, (202) 293-5968 (TDD), (202) 293-7999 (FAX). *That All May Worship: An Interfaith Welcome to People with Disabilities*. Washington, DC, 1992 (authors: Rose Ann Davie and Ginny Thornburgh).

National Rehabilitation Hospital, REquest Rehabilitation Engineering Center (REC), 102 Irving St., NW, Washington, DC 20010-2949, (202) 877-1932 (V), (202) 726-3996 (TDD), (202) 723-0628 (FAX). See Publications Order Form for product comparisons and evaluations, and other reports available from the Rehabilitation Engineering Center:
"A Selected Listing of Journals and Books on Assistive Technology."
"An Annotated Bibliography on Funding for Technology."
"Architectural Accessibility Resources"
"Evaluation of Assistive Technology."
"Information Centers and Clearinghouses."
"Mail Order Catalogs."
"Toll Free Numbers."
"Toward Universal Design: An Ongoing Project on the Ergonomics of Disability" (undated article by James Mueller).
"Workstation Design."

National Rehabilitation Information Center (NARIC), 8455 Colesville Rd., Suite 935, Silver Spring, MD 20910-3319, (800) 346-2742, (301) 588-9284, (301) 587-1967 (FAX), (301) 589-3563 (electronic bulletin board). Clearinghouse for numerous publications pertaining to all aspects of disabilities, available on two databases, reports, etc.:
ABLEDATA
REHABDATA
NARIC Quarterly
"Research and Training Centers"
"Rehabilitation Engineering Centers"
"Information Dissemination and Utilization Projects"
"Rehab Briefs" (prepared by PSI International, Falls Church, VA)

Paralyzed Veterans of America/Paradigm Design Group, 801 18th St., NW, Washington, DC 20006, (202) 416-7645:
Fair Housing Design Guide for Accessibility, Washington, D.C. 1992 (authors: Thomas D. Davies, Jr., AIA and Kim A. Beasley, AIA).
Design for Hospitality: Planning for Accessible Hotels and Motels. New York: Nichols Publishing, 1988 (authors: Thomas D. Davies, Jr., AIA and Kim A. Beasley, AIA).

Perkins School for the Blind, 175 North Beacon St., Watertown, MA 02172, (617) 924-3434. Library has several publications on adapting the environment for people who are visually disabled or blind.

President's Committee on Employment of People with Disabilities, 1331 F St., NW, 3rd floor, Washington, DC 20004, (202) 376-6200 (V), (202) 376-6205 (TDD), (202) 376-6219 (FAX) (*see also* United States . . .):
"Employers Are Asking . . . About Making the Workplace Accessible to Workers with Disabilities" (no date).
"Resources You Can Use: Resources Available to Supplement Your ADA Community Training" (no date).

RESNA (Association for the Advancement of Rehabilitation and Assistive Technology), 1101 Connecticut Ave., NW, Washington, DC 20036, (202) 857-1199, (202) 775-2625. Publication List and Assistive Technology Sourcebook.

Shrout, Richard Neil, *Resource Directory for the Disabled.* New York: Facts on File, 1991.

Spina Bifida Association of America, 1700 Rockville Pike, Suite 540, Rockville, MD 20525, (800) 621-3141, (301) 770-7222.

United Cerebral Palsy Association, 1522 K St., NW, Suite 1112, Washington, DC 20005, (800) USA-5UCP, (202) 842-1266 (V/TDD).

United States Department of Agriculture, Forest Service, Recreation Cultural and Wilderness Management, P. O. Box 96090, Washington, DC 20090-6090, (202) 205-1129:

Challenges to Opportunities: Accessibility for All (videotape).

"Design Guide for Accessible Outdoor Recreation" (currently out of print), Interim Draft for Review, September 1990, prepared by Interagency Guidelines Task Group for Accessible Outdoor Recreation, joint Forest Service and National Park Service effort, with Forest Service responsible for final guide.

United States Architectural and Transportation Barriers Compliance Board (Access Board), 1331 F St., NW, Suite 1000, Washington, DC 20004-1111, (800) USA-ABLE, (202) 272-5434 (V), (202) 272-5449 (TDD), (202) 272-5447 (FAX):

Federal Register, Friday Sept. 6, 1991, Part II, 36 CFR Part 1191, "Americans with Disabilities Act (ADA) Accessibility Guidelines for Buildings and Facilities; Amendment to Final Guidelines."

"Access America," newsletter of the Access Board.

United States Department of Education, Office of Special Education and Rehabilitative Services, National Institute on Disability and Rehabilitative Research, Washington, DC 20202-2524, (202) 205-8134:

"Summary of Existing Legislation Affecting Persons with Disabilities," August 1988, publication no. E-88-22014. Prepared by National Association of State Mental Retardation Program Directors, Inc.

"NIDRR Program Directory, Fiscal Year 1990."

United States Department of Housing and Urban Development, Office of HUD Program Compliance, Room 5204, H.U.D., 451 7th St., SW, Washington, DC 20410-0500, (202) 708-2618 (V), (202) 708-0015 (TDD). *Federal Register*, Wednesday, March 6, 1991, Part VI, Dept. of H.U.D., Office of the Assistant Secretary for Fair Housing and Equal Opportunity, 24 CFR Chapter 1, Final Fair Housing Accessibility Guidelines.

United States Department of Justice, Office on the Americans with Disabilities Act, Civil Rights Division, Washington, DC 20530, ADA Information Line (open 1 to 5 p.m., eastern time) (202) 514-0301 (V), (202) 514-0383 (TDD):

Federal Register, July 26, 1991, Part III, Department of Justice, Office of the Attorney General, 28 CFR Part 36, Nondiscrimination on the Basis of Disability by Public Accommodations and in Commercial Facilities: Final Rule, Appendix A to Part 36, ADA Accessibility Guidelines for Buildings and Facilities.

Title II (Public Services) of ADA complaints are filed with: Coordination and Review Section, Civil Rights Division, U.S. Department of Justice, P.O. Box 66118, Washington, DC 20035-6118.

Title III (Public Accommodations and Services Operated by Private Entitities) of ADA complaints are filed with: Public Access Section, Civil Rights Division, U.S. Department of Justice, P.O. Box 66738, Washington, DC 20035-9998.

United States Department of the Interior, National Park Service, Special Programs and Populations Branch, P.O. Box 37127, Washington, DC 20013-7127, (202) 343-3674:

Design, Winter and Fall issues, 1989

CRM Supplement, 1991, bulletin published by the Cultural Resources Branch, National Park Service, with input from Special Programs and Populations Branch.

United States Department of Transportation, 400 7th St., SW, Washington, DC 20590, (202) 366-4859:

Federal Register, Friday September 6, 1991, "Part IV, Department of Transportation, 49 CFR Parts 27, 37 and 38, Transportation for Individuals with Disabilities: Final Rule"

New Horizons for the Air Traveler with a Disability, Office of the Secretary, December 1991.

ADA Paratransit Handbook: Implementing the Complementary Paratransit Service Requirements of the Americans with Disabilities Act of 1990, prepared for the Urban Mass Transportation Agency Task Force on the Americans with Disabilities Act, Sept. 1991, UMTA-MA-06-0206-91-1.

Universal Designers & Consultants, Inc., 1700 Rockville Pike, Suite 110, Rockville, MD 20852, (301) 770–7890 (V/TDD), (301) 770–4338 (FAX). In addition to the booklets and articles written by John Salmen, AIA, president of the company, Universal Designers & Consultants conducts seminars, produces and distributes videotapes on ADA and accessible design, produces the quarterly "Universal Design Newsletter," and distributes other companies' publications pertaining to the ADA and accessible design issues.

Volunteers for Medical Engineering, 5202 Westland Blvd, Baltimore, MD 21227, (410) 455–6395.

LIST OF ARCHITECTS AND DESIGNERS

Alderstein, Michael, AIA
  NPS/Ellis Island
Architect of the Capitol (George
    White, FAIA)
  *United States Capitol & Supreme
    Court*
A.W. Landscapes
  residence
Beyer Blinder Belle
  Ellis Island
Beasley, Kim, AIA
  PVA, Orioles' Park Equal Access Seat
Buckley, Davis, AIA
  *National Law Enforcement Officers
    Memorial*
Clark, Thomas, AIA
  Resnik School
Cliver, Blaine, AIA
  NPS/Statue of Liberty
Corva, Angelo Francis, AIA
  Henry Viscardi School
Daly, Leo A.
  EEOC
Dawson, Stuart, FASLA
  *Waterfront Park, Enid A. Haupt
    Garden*
Desoorkian, Lida, IBD
  EEOC
Dynes, Susan
  apartment
Edward Pinckney Associates
  Waterfront Park
Erickson, Bill
  Shakespeare Theatre

Fields, Michael, AIA
  Gallaudet University
Frank, Lawrence V., ASLA
  residence
Franz, Anna Young, AIA
  Great Hall at Justice
Geier Brown Renfrow
  *Historical Society of Washington,
    Gallaudet University*
Graham Gund Architects
  Shakespeare Theatre
HOK Sports Facilities Group
  Orioles Park
JI, Inc. (Magneta, Yglesias, ASID)
  residence
(The) Landscape Group, Inc.
  Washington Home and Hospice
Lemieux, John
  residence
Mackler, Steve
  Washington Home and Hospice
Madden, Dennis
  St. Elizabeth
Madsen, Peter, FAIA
  Shakespeare Theatre
Mariani, Ted, FAIA
  National Rehabilitation Hospital
May, Arthur, FAIA
  *American Association of Retired
    Persons*
MetaForm
  Ellis Island and Statue of Liberty
Meyers, Alan, AIA
  Vice President's residence

INDEX